**DO NOT REMOVE
CARDS FROM POCKET**

Jennifer Rogers

A FIRESIDE BOOK
PUBLISHED BY
SIMON & SCHUSTER
NEW YORK LONDON TORONTO
SYDNEY TOKYO SINGAPORE

TRIED

and

TROUSSEAU

THE

BRIDE

GUIDE

FIRESIDE
Simon & Schuster Building
Rockefeller Center
1230 Avenue of the Americas
New York, New York 10020

Designed by Bonni Leon

Manufactured in the United States of America

10 9 8 7 6 5 4 3 2 1

Library of Congress Cataloging in Publication Data
Rogers, Jennifer, date
    Tried and trousseau: the bride guide/Jennifer Rogers.
        p. cm.
    "A Fireside book."
    Includes index.
    1. Weddings—Planning.   2. Weddings—United States—
Planning.   3. Weddings—Miscellanea.   I. Title.
HQ745.R64   1992
395'.22—dc20   91-29589
                                                                  CIP

ISBN 0-671-73935-2

Acknowledgments

Many brides and nonbrides helped with this project. I'm especially grateful to my editor, Kara Leverte, and to Barbara Plumb and Sol Skolnick, who were in on the book from the beginning. Thanks also to: Ann Amernick, Patience Beer, Jean Borash, Nancie B. Cameron, Mary Carden, Sue Carden, Tony Cook, Barbara Corvino, Emery Davis, Patty Delagar, Demetrios, Randi Diamond, Suzanne Donahue, Andrea Dukakis, Robbi Ernst, Karen Faircloth, Al Falkowski, Steven Feinberg, Edna Forsyth, Mia Freund, Laura Freundlich, Arthur Frommer, Kristina Garvin, Kelly Gladder, Arlene Grasso, Lee Gruzen, Hannelore Hahn, Jane Harnick, Claire Heffernan, Kate Heffernan, Michael Herman, Shawna Hicks, Janet Hill, Michelle Hinkson, Bea Hoelle, Deborah Hughes, Eileen Jordan, Deborah Keane, Charles Kreloff, Beth Kulok, Susan Lane, Mark Laporta, Timothy Lee, Michelle Lehnen, Bonni Leon, Eve MacGrath, Mary Manning, Patty Marx, Lydia May, Julie Merberg, Pattie Miller, Jerry Monaghan, Lisa Montenegro, Joyce Nalepka, Deborah O'Flynn, Bo Parker, Nancy Parramore, Jackie Pash, Mary Ellen Petrikat, Vincent Piccione, Tom Pirko, Betsy Radin, Lyn Ramsey, Carolyn Sadler, Hedda Schacter, Peter Schiffman, Jay Schweitzer, Stanley Selengut, Jackie Seow, Becky Sikes, Lisa Sims, Deborah Skolnik, Sarah Skolnik, Annena Sorenson, Marilyn Spiegel, Bernie Toll, Ben Trautman, Vera Wang, Ben Weinstock, Sylvia Weinstock, Adrienne Welles, Terence Womble, David Yassky, and Memo Zack.

For my mother and father

CONTENTS

10

12

Seven

THE GETAWAY

Being and Becoming *211*

Eight

16

Invitation

he honor of your presence is requested at your own wedding. So what if you're getting on in years, have been through this before, or absolutely need to be back at the office on Monday morning? Every bride, whatever her circumstances, is entitled to revel in the oldest surviving rite of passage (including fraternity hazing) known to man.

Tried and Trousseau mirrors the elements that all weddings everywhere have shared from pagan times to the present no matter the price range: the procession, the presentation of a specially costumed bride, the ceremony, the feast, the getaway. The book offers a historical perspective that will bring new meaning to your wedding—and all the need-to-know information that will help you with the proposal, rings, engagement announcements, invitations, showers, the rehearsal dinner, your gown, your attendants, your bridal consultant, the vows, the receiving line, the toasts, the florists, bakers, photographers, musicians, your mother, and more. Much more. If, like a dream, a wedding is the same but different every time it occurs, so also is it open to interpretation. These pages show you how to decode the age-old universal tradition of the princess bride and fit it to your most up-to-date and personal wishes.

Regally, serenely, you will learn how to get your picture in *The New York Times;* make your little brother feel important because he's addressing envelopes; deal with blended families, corporate culture, gender politics. You'll reign supremely confident over everything from the recitation of the passage from *Walden* to dancing to music from *The Big Chill.* Evenhandedly, capably, you will settle disputes about the origins of the diamond engagement ring, the true significance of hurled rice, the best champagne to serve, the hour the videographer was supposed to arrive. In short, with the help of this book, your crown should rest more easily on your head all the way from engagement to honeymoon.

So keep on dreaming. No one (including you) has ever had a wedding quite like the one you envision. Earlier events may have been triumphs of the barter system, or lyrical enactments of romance, or memorable examples of a time when the flowers really got out of hand (see the wedding of President Grover Cleveland, page 30), but centuries of bridal pageants have yet to prepare the world for what you intend. If you're having a big blowout it may take you a year to plan the day; even if you're having a smaller or simpler celebration you must organize. No need to panic. The answers are here. Simply follow those who have gone before—as you lead the way.

TRIED

and

TROUSSEAU

Chapter One

WHAT'S BARBARISM GOT TO DO WITH IT?

GETTING

ORIENTED

ontemporary wedding ceremonies have origins in the prehistoric practice of *marriage by capture*, wherein the young men of one tribe invaded the camp of another tribe and stole the bride. The groom's friends were along to make sure no one stopped them—neither the bride's girlfriends, who did the best they could to save her, nor her father, who tended to become so enraged he threw things. This organized melee continued for centuries, gradually evolving into organized business. With *marriage by purchase* the young warriors of one tribe might invade the camp of another—but now it was to suggest to the bride's father that the groom was willing to pay something for her. This was the "wed-price" or "wed" and it's the origin of the word "wedding." The groom's go-betweens proposed that the bride's father could gain money, livestock, and/or other property in the deal, so long as the bride brought to the marriage her virginity and a "dowry" of all her worldly goods. Bargaining proceeded over these points. The bride stood by as chattel while everyone operated on the premise that a father deserved to be recompensed for all the work his daughter could have performed in the fields, if only she hadn't been carried off by her groom to *his* fields.

Hundreds of years went by. A proliferation of matchmakers and marriage brokers haggled over dowries and bride-prices and created alliances among tribes that would be echoed later in the alliances among nations created by royal weddings. Fathers gained in wealth and influence. Virginity became incredibly important. Grooms paid up. Rather than waiting to be kidnapped, as in the old days, brides began to journey to their grooms' villages, taking their "bridesmaids" along to protect their dowries, and themselves, from robbers.

Medieval times arrived. The rise of the Roman Catholic Church allowed St. Augustine to insist that mutual agreement, not rape or riches, made for the truer marriage. Even though dowries continued to exist, something new took hold: *marriage by consent*, in which the bride had to say yes. After that, it was only a few hundred more years to *marriage for love*, an eighteenth-century development that appears to have been simultaneous with the stirrings of the middle class. As the Age of Enlightenment dawned, grooms wised up. Courtship replaced pillaging; a proposal, bodily attack.

Finally, there came modern times. Wedding gifts today are displayed like so much loot. Brides and grooms surround themselves with teams of friends. Fathers give their daughters away. Love is in the air. The more things change, the more they stay the same. Elements of all previous forms of marriage are preserved and refined in current rituals. Progress is on the march, and the beat goes on.

Wedding procession in ancient Rome.

HOW TO GET MARRIED IN ANCIENT ROME

Lay aside your childish toga praetexta. Dedicate your dolls to the family's divine spirits. Put on a tunic without a hem; fasten it with a woolen girdle tied with the Knot of Hercules. Put on a saffron-yellow cloak and sandals. Put on: a metal necklace; six pads of artificial hair (just like the Vestal Virgins); a red or yellow veil; a crown of orange blossoms. Join your family to welcome wedding guests. Stand by while someone kills a sheep or pig. Clasp hands over a flame with the groom while pledging yourselves to each other. Have a feast. March in a torchlight parade to your new home. Let the groom carry you over the threshold. Let him untie your Knot of Hercules.

VICTORIA AND HER DESCENDANTS

1837–1988

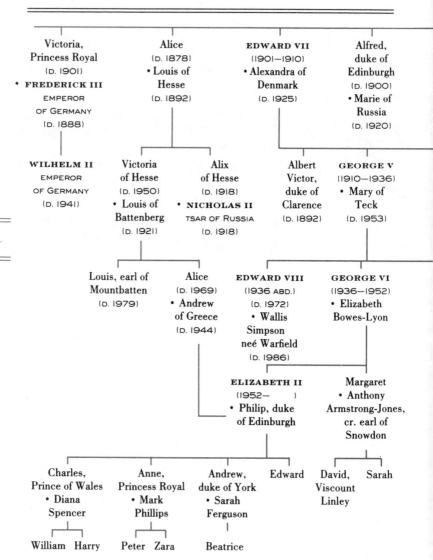

Victoria,
Princess Royal
(D. 1901)
• **FREDERICK III**
EMPEROR
OF GERMANY
(D. 1888)

Alice
(D. 1878)
• Louis of
Hesse
(D. 1892)

EDWARD VII
(1901—1910)
• Alexandra of
Denmark
(D. 1925)

Alfred,
duke of
Edinburgh
(D. 1900)
• Marie of
Russia
(D. 1920)

WILHELM II
EMPEROR
OF GERMANY
(D. 1941)

Victoria
of Hesse
(D. 1950)
• Louis of
Battenberg
(D. 1921)

Alix
of Hesse
(D. 1918)
• **NICHOLAS II**
TSAR OF RUSSIA
(D. 1918)

Albert
Victor,
duke of
Clarence
(D. 1892)

GEORGE V
(1910—1936)
• Mary of
Teck
(D. 1953)

24

Louis, earl of
Mountbatten
(D. 1979)

Alice
(D. 1969)
• Andrew
of Greece
(D. 1944)

EDWARD VIII
(1936 ABD.)
(D. 1972)
• Wallis
Simpson
neé Warfield
(D. 1986)

GEORGE VI
(1936—1952)
• Elizabeth
Bowes-Lyon

ELIZABETH II
(1952—   )
• Philip, duke
of Edinburgh

Margaret
• Anthony
Armstrong-Jones,
cr. earl of
Snowdon

Charles,
Prince of Wales
• Diana
Spencer

Anne,
Princess Royal
• Mark
Phillips

Andrew,
duke of York
• Sarah
Ferguson

Edward

David,
Viscount
Linley

Sarah

William   Harry

Peter   Zara

Beatrice

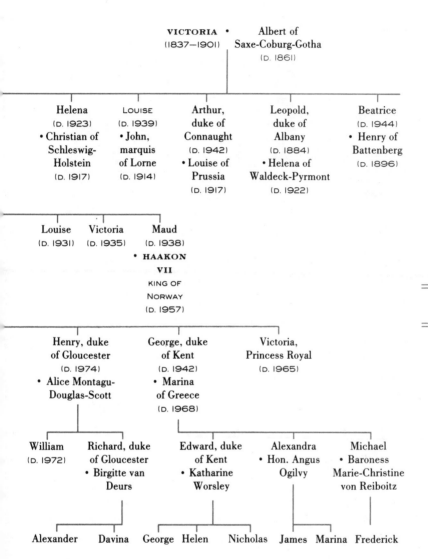

VICTORIA • Albert of
(1837–1901) Saxe-Coburg-Gotha
(D. 1861)

Helena
(D. 1923)
• Christian of
Schleswig-
Holstein
(D. 1917)

LOUISE
(D. 1939)
• John,
marquis
of Lorne
(D. 1914)

Arthur,
duke of
Connaught
(D. 1942)
• Louise of
Prussia
(D. 1917)

Leopold,
duke of
Albany
(D. 1884)
• Helena of
Waldeck-Pyrmont
(D. 1922)

Beatrice
(D. 1944)
• Henry of
Battenberg
(D. 1896)

Louise
(D. 1931)

Victoria
(D. 1935)

Maud
(D. 1938)
• HAAKON
VII
KING OF
NORWAY
(D. 1957)

Henry, duke
of Gloucester
(D. 1974)
• Alice Montagu-
Douglas-Scott

George, duke
of Kent
(D. 1942)
• Marina
of Greece
(D. 1968)

Victoria,
Princess Royal
(D. 1965)

William
(D. 1972)

Richard, duke
of Gloucester
• Birgitte van
Deurs

Edward, duke
of Kent
• Katharine
Worsley

Alexandra
• Hon. Angus
Ogilvy

Michael
• Baroness
Marie-Christine
von Reiboitz

Alexander   Davina   George   Helen   Nicholas   James   Marina   Frederick

BETTMANN ARCHIVE

Queen Victoria and Prince Albert at the time of their marriage.

THE ORIGINAL VICTORIAN ROMANCE

Today, the way to spell romance is with a V for Victoria. The queen whose marriage to her prince brought new luster not only to England but to the universal cause of love sent this note to Albert on the morning they were to be married:

10 February 1840

How are you today, and have you slept well? I have rested very well, and feel very comfortable today. What weather! I believe, however, the rain will cease. Send one word when you, my most dearly loved bridegroom, will be ready. Thy ever faithful, Victoria R.

PERTINENT FACTS ABOUT QUEEN VICTORIA'S CHILDREN

ONE POWERFUL BRIDE

The marriage, in 1840, of Britain's Queen Victoria to Albert of Saxe-Coburg-Gotha produced nine offspring; their marriages in turn created liaisons that strengthened the royal houses of Europe politically and economically for generations to come.

Queen Victoria and her family.

There were nine of them. They and their children influenced the course of world affairs well into the twentieth century. They were:

VICTORIA *b. 1840, d. 1901 ("Vicky")*. The firstborn. Her title was Princess Royal. She was not an heir to the throne. Described as "merry, bright, and affectionate," but "given to tantrums." She carried hemophilia (inherited from Victoria R., who didn't know she carried it at the time of her marriage). Married the Prince of Prussia and gave birth to the future Kaiser of Germany.

ALBERT *b. 1841, d. 1910 ("Bertie")*. Ascended the throne of England as Edward VII. Described as "backward, idle, rude, violent, and dull." It was for Bertie that the first little boy's sailor suit was made. He married into the Royal House of Denmark.

ALICE *b. 1843, d. 1878*. Had a very sweet nature. Was close to Bertie and something of a peacemaker in the family. Carried hemophilia. Married Louis of Hesse.

ALFRED *b. 1844, d. 1900*. Musical. In the Navy. Married Grand Duchess Marie of Russia.

HELENA *b. 1846, d. 1923*. Clever. Amiable. Ugly. She married Christian of Schleswig-Holstein.

LOUISE *b. 1848, d. 1939*. Artistic and pretty. Married John Campbell, the ninth Duke of Argyll.

ARTHUR *b. 1850, d. 1942*. The favorite child. He joined the Royal Military Academy at the age of seventeen. Married Princess Louise Margaret of Prussia.

LEOPOLD *b. 1853, d. 1884*. Smart but unattractive. A hemophiliac. He married Helena, Princess of Waldeck-Pyrmont.

BEATRICE *b. 1857, d. 1944*. She was precocious, but after her father died became very shy. Carried hemophilia. Married Prince Henry of Battenberg.

—based on Celia Clear's *Royal Children*
(Crown Publishers)

Which is more important: the royal heirs or the dynastic marriage? Is it the first task of a royal to perpetuate himself or to create an alliance? Let the anthropologists argue. Meanwhile, be thankful you're not marrying a king (if you're not). You'd probably be truly nervous. How could you help it, with the whole world watching?

In addition to Queen Victoria and Prince Albert's 1840 nuptials, these royal weddings stick in memory:

1990: Prince Aya of Japan to commoner Kiko Kawashima

1986: Andrew, Duke of York, to publishing employee Sarah Ferguson

1981: Charles, Prince of Wales, to Lady Diana Spencer

1978: King Hussein of Jordan to Princeton graduate Lisa Halaby

1963: Then Crown Prince Maharajkumar Thondup Namgyal of Sikkim to socialite Hope Cooke

1953: Prince Rainier of Monaco to movie star Grace Kelly

1947: Princess Elizabeth to the Duke of Edinburgh

1937: The Duke of Windsor (formerly King Edward VIII) to divorcée Wallis Warfield Simpson

Polls show that the President's popularity skyrockets the day after a White House wedding. Some unions that won the union's approval:

WHITE HOUSE OCCUPANT	MARRIED TO	YEAR	MEMORABLE ASPECTS
JOHN ADAMS	Mary Catherine Hellen	1828	The only presidential son ever to marry in the White House, he was the son of John Quincy Adams and the grandson of John Adams. She was his cousin. The President disapproved of the match because the bride had flirted with the groom's brothers.
GROVER CLEVELAND	Frances Folsom	1866	She was the daughter of his deceased law partner, and had been his ward since age eleven. (See page 209 for their floral decorations.)
NELLIE GRANT	Algernon Sartoris	1874	They had a seven-course wedding feast, and Walt Whitman wrote a poem for the bride.

WHITE HOUSE OCCUPANT	MARRIED TO	YEAR	MEMORABLE ASPECTS
ALICE ROOSEVELT	Nicholas Longworth	1906	She had no bridesmaids, so her cousin Franklin Delano Roosevelt held her train (and later became President).
LUCI BAINES JOHNSON	Patrick Nugent	1966	She was the first presidential daughter to be married in a Catholic ceremony, and in a church; she took some of her wedding cake with her on her honeymoon to the Bahamas.
LYNDA BIRD JOHNSON	Charles Robb	1967	He was the very good-looking White House marine guard and future senator from Virginia who plucked her away from actor George Hamilton.
TRICIA NIXON	Edward Cox	1971	The recipe for her lemon sponge wedding cake was released to a trusting, pre-Watergate, press— who published it without testing it. Soon, the citizenry was trying to bake a cake that wouldn't become cake. A corrected version of the recipe was subsequently provided by the White House.

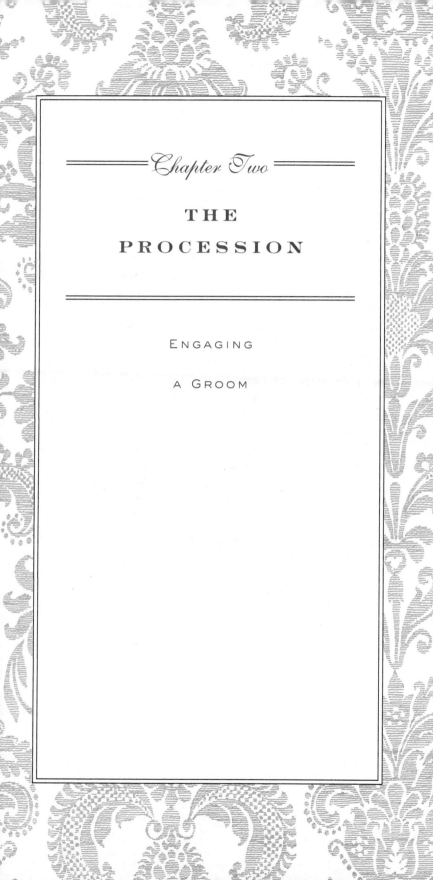

Chapter Two

THE
PROCESSION

ENGAGING

A GROOM

THE HAND THEY SHAKE
MAY BE YOUR OWN

When He Asks Your Father's
Permission to Wed

 n keeping with the earliest traditions of marriage, over the years the groom has requested the hand of the bride from her father. This transfer of power has reportedly pleased both men, as it seems so much more refined than selling the bride for cold cash. Indeed, as weddings evolved through the centuries, some fathers and grooms merely repaired to the elder's all-male club, where they held a stilted conversation that sealed the bride's fate forever. This usually happened when she wasn't looking—behind her back, you might say. The custom was protocol at its most intriguing. Probably, she didn't even know they were intending to have drinks together! In recent years, most all-male eating clubs have been directed by the courts to admit females, however. And that's not all that's changed. Today's bride may have been raised by her divorced mother, and there may have been a stepfather in the picture. Grooms who persist in asking paternal permission to wed (it can be a fairly emotional encounter) are advised to be considerate of others. Including the bride. Does it bother her to be up for auction? Not noticeably. She thinks of it this way: Boys will be boys. It's nice they care.

When He Asks Your Permission to Wed

he proposal is the most excellent of all questions. It implies its answer—not to mention a future, possible children, a wedding to plan. The basic proposal is "Will you marry me?" but countless are the ways and sites in which the proposal has been articulated, and various the media that have carried it. Current trends point to creative use of small machines: fax and video proposals are on the rise. Everywhere, the emphasis is on creativity. A fortune cookie may contain a specially printed message, an electronic sign the request for an instant reply. Messengers are dispatched through urban streets and avenues; beach-goers basking in the sun look up and read the skywriting. Proposals occur on land, sea, and in the air. They happen at such public places as the observation deck atop the Empire State Building, or at home—where a woman living with her boyfriend may open the refrigerator to find an engagement ring inside. You don't have to have a ring to make a proposal, however. A good proposal needs only words—spoken, written, or other (one groom hired a sidewalk mime)—that come from the heart. Proposals happen at parties, at work, at the gym, at

INTRIGUING NEW TRENDS IN PROPOSALS

- Sending them via E-mail on CompuServe.
- Waiting until the (practically unconscious) bride has just completed running a marathon.
- Taking the real estate approach: whether to renew the lease depends on the proposal's outcome.
- Working backward: whipping out a Filofax to set a wedding date implies the proposal.
- Tampering with a Cracker Jack box, to hide a diamond ring inside as the "prize."
- Sending an airline ticket to the bride; after she's seated on the plane, taking the place next to her and answering the question "What are you doing here?" with another question: "Will you marry me?" (The engagement is

someone else's wedding. They come at the best or worst possible time—and when they're · most or least expected. They can be studies in flattery, or works of self-consciousness; simple queries, or an opportunity for wit. The proposal launches the engagement (average length in the United States today: 11.6 months). And, more important, the proposal is the true beginning of the wedding.

announced over the plane's loudspeaker during takeoff.)
• Hiking to the top of a mountain together, to ask the question at the summit.
• Pasting an engagement ring into a lavish full-color art book about crown jewels.
• Trick-or-treating the bride on Halloween.
• Hiding the ring somewhere in a state park; inviting guests to a rigged treasure hunt.
• Slipping the ring onto a shrimp during the appetizer course.
• The bride does the asking (a whopping 90 percent of resulting marriages survive, according to a study).

JUST SAY YES

Ronald Reagan Proposes to Nancy Davis in Hollywood

And one night over dinner as we sat at a table for two, I said, "Let's get married." She deserved a more romantic proposal than that, but—bless her—she put her hand on mine, looked into my eyes, and said, "Let's."
—Ronald Reagan, *An American Life*

JAMES JOYCE AND THE YES PASSAGE FROM *ULYSSES*

If the wedding truly begins the moment the bride says yes to the proposal, it may be well to consider how most perfectly to say that word. James Joyce brought new meaning to it in Ulysses. Was he thinking of someone special at the time he composed the famous "yes" passage? Joyce student Sarah Skolnik provides background:

They were both in their early thirties; both slept with their husbands in the same inverted positions, head to toe; and both could boast of sexual experiences at the age of fifteen. They were both jealous of their rapidly maturing adolescent daughters and both called their husbands by a cherished nickname, reserved only for them. Both dabbled on stage. Both, as young girls, had a boyfriend named Mulvey. Both hated umbrellas, liked roast chicken, read pornography, and believed in God. Molly Bloom, the character who utters the profound affirmation of love and marriage at the end of *Ulysses*, bears a striking resemblance to James Joyce's wife, Nora Barnacle.

Nora, however, adamantly rejected the idea that her husband had merely painted her portrait in his final chapter, consistently dismissing the fictional Molly as a "big, fat, horrible married woman . . . much fatter" than she. And in some ways the Molly/Nora comparison does fall short. Molly's famous "yes I said yes I will Yes" offers an enthusiastic view of matrimony long absent in the Joyce household. James Joyce rejected the institution of marriage and only proposed to Nora Barnacle after they had lived together for twenty-seven years and had two grown children. "Why should I have brought Nora to a priest or a lawyer to make

James and Nora Joyce.

her swear away her life to me?" he asked for many years before finally marrying her in a civil ceremony in 1931.

Nora, who once called her husband's work "that chop suey you're writing," and pled with him to "write sensible books that people can understand," nevertheless had followed the brooding writer onto an oceanliner when she was only twenty years old, running away to Zurich without a marriage proposal, or even the promise of one anytime soon. "No other human being has stood so close to my soul as you stand," Joyce told her, but he wouldn't say he loved her.

They'd met only months before, on Nassau Street in Dublin, where the grossly nearsighted Joyce, walking without his glasses, could barely see Nora and nearly knocked her over. After that, she penned impassioned love letters, writing in the same fevered, rambling style that characterizes Molly's monologue, planning clandestine meetings or teasing Joyce with erotic fantasies. Upon his request, Nora carried Joyce's return letters into bed with her —just as Molly reads her missive from Blazes Boylan in bed.

Many scholars have suggested that Joyce and Nora enjoyed their first date on June 16, 1904, the day on which all the action in *Ulysses* takes place. Richard Ellman, Joyce's most respected biographer, believes that "to set *Ulysses* on this date was Joyce's most eloquent, if indirect, tribute to Nora."

the day I got him to propose to me yes first I gave him the bit of seedcake out of my mouth and it was leapyear like now yes 16 years ago my God after that long kiss I near lost my breath yes he *said I was a flower of the mountain yes so we are flowers all a womans body yes that was one true thing he said in his life and the sun shines for you today yes that was why I liked him because I saw he understood or felt what a woman is and I knew I could always get round him and I gave him all the pleasure I could leading him on till he asked me to say yes and I wouldnt answer first only looked out over the sea and the sky I was thinking of so many things he didnt know of Mulvey and Mr Stanhope and Hester and father and old captain Groves and the sailors playing all birds fly and I say stoop and washing up dishes they called it on the pier and the sentry in front of the governors house with the thing round his white helmet poor devil half roasted and the Spanish girls laughing in their shawls and their tall combs and the auctions in the morning the Greeks and the Jews and the Arabs and the devil knows who else from all the ends of Europe and Duke Street and the fowl market all clucking outside Larby Sharons and the poor donkeys slipping half asleep and the vague fellows in the cloaks asleep in the shade on the steps and the big wheels of the carts of the bulls and the old castle thousands of years old yes and those handsome Moors all in white and turbans like kings asking you to sit down in their little bit of a shop and Ronda with the old windows of the posadas glancing eyes a lattice hid for her lover to kiss the iron and the wineshops half open at night and the castanets and the night we missed the boat at Algeciras the watchman going about serene with his lamp and O that awful deep-down torrent O and the sea the sea crimson sometimes like fire and the glorious sunsets and the figtrees in the Alameda gardens yes and all the queer little streets and the pink and blue and yellow houses and the rosegardens and the jessamine and geraniums and cactuses and Gibraltar as a girl where I was a Flower of the mountain yes when I put the rose in my hair like the Andalusian girls used or shall I wear a red yes and how he kissed me under the Moorish wall and I thought well as well him as another and then I asked him with my eyes to ask again yes and then he asked me would I yes to say yes my mountain flower and first I put my arms around him yes and drew him down to me so he could feel my breasts all perfume yes and his heart was going like mad and yes I said yes I will Yes.**

—James Joyce, Ulysses*

The Prenuptial Agreement

egal Valentine or legal death warrant? Argument rages as to just how icky a prenuptial agreement is —or isn't—but the number of such contracts is increasing. There are at least twice as many (and probably more) today as there were in the mid-1980s. And it's not just among the non-down-and-out in Beverly Hills that they're so popular. Not just among movie stars, that is—not just among the rich and famous and the citizens of California, who are bound by that state's famous community property laws (husband and wife each get 50 percent at the time of divorce, no matter who earned what).

But everywhere. Recognized in all fifty states, prenups are gaining in popularity with the middle and upwardly mobile classes. Here are the people most likely to use them:

- Couples making $50,000 and up
- Couples over age thirty (who may have substantial assets by now)
- Couples with children from a previous marriage (who wish to protect their property)
- Couples in interfaith marriages (who wish to predetermine their children's religion)
- Two-income couples who wish to spell out the conditions under which one will relocate for the other's career

There are two kinds of prenuptial agreements—financial and "lifestyle." Often, one leads to the other; usually, the two are incorporated into the same document (which may run to fifty or even one hundred pages in length).

1 FINANCIAL. When one spouse is just way richer than the other, he or she may want to protect specific assets in the event of divorce or death; similarly, a bride or groom who expects to inherit family money may feel a fiduciary responsibility toward the generations to come. Far and away the chief reason for a financial prenuptial, though, has to do with one simple statistic:

in 45 percent of all new marriages one or both of the partners has been married before. These couples are apt to bring to their new union not only significant property that, by definition, was not accumulated together, but also children. Thus the contract is made to ensure the maintenance of certain living standards and expectations of inheritance. It is drawn up only after full financial disclosure by both the bride and groom, and labels and earmarks the funds somewhat in the manner of a last will and testament; who gets what—still and eventually—is settled from the get-go. (A typical formula: bride and groom keep their premarital assets separate and agree to split everything else evenly should they divorce.) Supposedly, as with any good business transaction, everyone benefits, if only because tension is removed. As poet Robert Frost said, "Good fences make good neighbors."

2 LIFESTYLE. Again, couples who have been married before may believe if only they'd been smarter . . . Well, this time they will be! They think of everything—religion, household chores, money, sex, in-laws, how many times a week they will dine together—and spell out how each issue will be handled in the marriage. Are these lifestyle agreements enforceable? Maybe, maybe not. Probably not.

Couples are cautioned not to bring up the topic of a prenuptial agreement for the first time while in bed, but if you ultimately do decide it's more romantic to throw your lots in together separately, as it were, and want to go ahead, heed this advice from lawyers in the field:

• Bride and groom should hire separate counsel.
• Bride and groom should each disclose finances, in separate statements.
• Bride and groom should each carefully read the letter sent by the other side's attorney; this tool of the trade among lawyers who write prenuptial agreements is intended to prevent a malpractice suit later by letting the signee know exactly what rights he or she has waived.
• A court reporter should attend the signing of the contract, and/or the signing of the contract should be videotaped.

PHOTO COURTESY MARVIN MITCHELSON

Marvin Mitchelson, the father of the prenuptial agreement.

WRAPPING HIM AROUND
YOUR LITTLE . . . THUMB

Origins of the Engagement Ring

I f, as a wife, you think wearing two rings on one finger is redundant, you're right—historically speaking, at least. The wedding band, given during the exchange of vows, is a relatively new phenomenon. Look back over the centuries, and you'll find the bride seemingly content to wear the one and only ring her groom ever gave her. She got her *betrothal ring* at the time of her engagement, well before the ceremony. It didn't feature a gemstone; it was simple, even plain. Only as times (and the church) changed did a second ring appear and today's engagement ring become the first of two. Some say the ring's symbolism goes all the way back to marriage by capture—that it stands for the grasses used to tie the bride's ankles and wrists to prevent her from running away. Others say the ring is rooted in marriage by purchase—that it's merely the bride-price in disguise, and that even the most primitive rings, of plaited rushes, symbolized the groom's ownership of the bride.

When romantics speak of the endless circle of love that has neither beginning nor end, they may or may not have in mind certain notable forerunners of the contemporary engagement ring. **ANCIENT GREEK AND ROMAN RINGS.** They were made of iron and other hand-wrought metals, an evolutionary step up from the straw,

The ring given by Archduke Maximilian to Mary of Burgundy is the earliest known example of a diamond ring given to seal an engagement.

leather, stone, and animal bone of earlier times. In Roman culture, the ring was used as a seal to signify the woman's duty to preserve the goods of her husband, as the care of the house belonged to her. Some of the rings had little knobs in the form of a key—not so much to symbolize how capable she was of unlocking the secrets of her husband's soul as how free she was to open his storehouse and help herself to a bag of grain or a roll of linen. Eventually, this ring came to have a dangling heart, the groom's way of saying "Everything I own belongs to you."

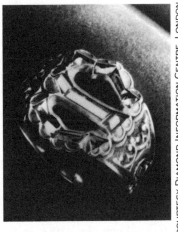

A copy of a ring in the Kunsthistorisches Museum in Vienna. Hogback diamonds, the forerunner of today's baguette, are arranged in the shape of the Gothic letter "M," alluding to the Virgin Mary.

MEDIEVAL RINGS.

Often worn on the bride's thumb, these rings might show clasped hands, or twin hearts pierced with Cupid's arrow, or a single heart in a loving hand. Saints' likenesses were popular, too. The early Christian church called the ring the *annulus pronubus;* it stood for the groom's pledge to wed, and the bride's pledge to keep herself for him alone. In Italy, artisans let their imaginations run: it was here, in the fifteenth century, that the diamond first appeared on the betrothal ring. Why a diamond? Because the beauty and hardness of the stone stood for the couple's strengthening devotion and enduring love. The diamonds in these rings reflected black, by the way—it wasn't until modern times that diamond cutters found ways to facet and polish the stone to catch the light.

THE GIMMAL. From the Latin word *gemelli,* for twins. This was the original double ring, popular during the sixteenth and seventeenth centuries in Europe. How it worked: two hoops could be clasped together for one apparently solid ring; however, separating the rings allowed one to be given to each lover. (Modern-day grooms who wear wedding rings just like their brides' can probably thank the gimmal.) The gimmal obviously alluded to the marriage bond; this allusion was highlighted by inscriptions taken from the text of the Christian marriage ceremony and engraved inside the hoop. Martin Luther married Katharina von Bora with such a ring, on which was inscribed "Whom God has joined together let no man put asunder." Elaborate enamel work usually embellished the rings.

POSIE RINGS. The "posie" refers to poesy—to a little poem, not a little flower. Popular in Europe from the fourteenth to the eighteenth centuries, the posie ring had a loving and/or pious inscription hidden inside. Anne of Cleves, who married Henry VIII, wore a posie ring that read "God send me well to kepe." Another inscription must have been cut in very small letters: "Love him who gave thee this ring of gold, For he must kiss thee When thou art old." (*Note:* Posie rings had precursors in antiquity. A Greek betrothal ring from about 400 B.C. bears a single word inside: "Honey.")

REGARD RINGS. Worn during the eighteenth century, they were studded with jewels, many jewels, and the jewels spelled a word. The lineup *R*uby *E*merald *G*arnet *A*methyst *R*uby *D*iamond spelled REGARD.

THE TIFFANY RING.

Maybe you're wearing one even as you read this? An American bridal tradition, this famous ring was created in the 1870s, shortly after the discovery of diamonds in South Africa. The Tiffany setting holds a solitaire in six tiny gold or platinum claws, a design that not only allows light to enter and leave the diamond from all sides, but also allows almost all of the gem to be seen. Thanks to this breakthrough, the emphasis of the modern engagement ring passed from the setting to the stone itself.

PHOTO COURTESY TIFFANY AND CO.

An engagement ring is a matter for serious thought on the part of the young man. The best that his pocket can afford is what he desires and a ring that will please his fiancee's taste is even more important. Either by asking her directly or from someone who knows her preferences he finds out her desire and tries in every way to fulfil it. The solitaire diamond as large and perfect as he could afford has for many years been the standard engagement ring.

—E. F. Cushing, Culture and Good Manners USA, 1926

"ONE BEAUTIFULLY JEWELED BAND." This is the most up-to-the-minute trend (and a quote from John Loring, design director for none other than Tiffany & Co.). Working women and young mothers, sometimes reluctant to wear a large stone that's cumbersome and easy to lose, are by popular demand bringing back historic practices. Asking for antique forms, as well as uniquely modern sculptural designs, they are once again wearing the single ring of their ancestors.

Don't Try This Alone

Why the third finger, left hand, for the ring(s)? Most historians think the custom stems from the Greeks, who believed there was an artery in the ring finger leading—sigh!—directly to the heart. Others contend the practice traces to medieval church ritual: when the groom touched three fingers of the bride's left hand in the name of the Trinity—"the Father, Son, and Holy Ghost"—the ring remained on the third finger for life. Still other experts maintain the third finger, left hand, is merely the sentimental choice—it's hard to lift independently.

Some grooms approach the job of acquiring a diamond engagement ring in much that way—as a job. They may wish to think of the following need-to-know information as a memo. Ready? To obtain a diamond of quality, consider:

CUT: Don't confuse cut with shape. A well-cut diamond is better able to handle light, creating more scintillation and sparkle.

COLOR: The best color for a diamond is no color. A totally colorless diamond best allows white light to pass effortlessly through it and be dispersed as rainbows of color.

CLARITY: Most diamonds contain very tiny natural marks known as inclusions. However, the fewer and smaller the inclusions are, the less likely it is that they will interfere with the passage of light through the diamond.

CARAT-WEIGHT: The weight of a diamond is measured in carats. One carat is divided into 100 points. So a diamond of 75 points weighs three-quarters of a carat.

Diamonds don't come in the shape of a diamond. They come in these shapes:

SHAPE	NAME	FAMOUS EXAMPLE
Circle	Brilliant	—
Heart	Heart	—
Pear	Pear	The "Indore Pears" given to an American heiress, in 1926, by an ex-Maharajah
Egg	Oval	The "Koh-i-nor," with Crown Jewels in Tower of London
Square	Princess	The "Red Cross Diamond"; it is yellow, was coveted by at least one prince of India, and its

		whereabouts are currently unknown
Elliptical	Marquise	The one owned by Madame de Pompadour, who was a marquise, duchess, and famed mistress of Louis XV
Rectangular	Emerald	The "Jonker Diamond" bought, in 1949, by King Farouk of Egypt

TEN THINGS TO KNOW
ABOUT DIAMONDS

1 Diamonds were first discovered in India, over two thousand years ago.

2 The word "diamond" comes from the ancient Greek word *adamas*, which means invincible. The diamond is so hard it can withstand fire and water.

3 The Greeks believed diamonds were the tears of the gods. The Romans thought of diamonds as splinters from falling stars.

4 The first diamond engagement ring was probably the one given to Mary of Burgundy, in 1477, by Archduke Maximilian of Austria.

5 The usual guideline for anyone about to buy an engagement ring: don't spend more than three weeks' salary, or 6 percent of your income. (*Note:* In the high-flying eighties, some people adjusted the guideline to a full two months' salary, but beware of investing too much; disreputable jewelers often inflate value. If you're eager to spend extra money, wait for your anniversary and buy an additional diamond then.)

6 A study conducted at the turn of the decade revealed that 70 percent of all brides received a diamond engagement ring, while 77 percent of first-time brides did.

7 Three-quarters of all engagement rings are selected by the couple together, rather than by the groom alone.

8 More than 35 percent of all engagement rings are presented during the three months at the end of the year.

9 The brilliant round solitaire diamond ring is the style most popular with American brides. Seventy-eight percent wear this model.

10 Diamond merchants have lots of opinions about the classic Dustin Hoffman/Laurence Olivier movie *Marathon Man.* Just ask.

FOUR EASY WAYS TO CLEAN DIAMONDS

1 THE DETERGENT BATH. Prepare a small bowl of warm suds with any of the mild liquid detergents used in the home. Brush the pieces with an eyebrow brush while they are in the suds, then rinse under warm running water. Pat dry with a soft, lint-free cloth.

PHOTO COURTESY DIAMOND INFORMATION CENTRE, LONDON

2 THE COLD WATER SOAK. Soak the jewelry in a half-and-half solution of cold water and household ammonia for thirty minutes. Lift out and gently tap around the front and back of the mounting with an eyebrow brush. Swish in the solution a second time and drain on tissue paper.

3 THE QUICK DIP METHOD. Use any of the brand-name liquid jewelry cleaners; follow the instructions on the label.

4 THE ULTRASONIC CLEANER. There are many ultrasonic machines on the market that will clean any piece of jewelry. The package consists of a machine with a metal cup that is to be filled with water and detergent. When the machine is turned on, a high-frequency turbulence creates the cleaning action. Each machine is different, so it is necessary to follow the accompanying directions.

YOUR ANNOUNCEMENT
AND THE RECORDED
ANNOUNCEMENT

Telling the Society Page About Your Engagement and Wedding

 ven the most reserved bridal couples are generally eager to shout their news to the world. That's why there are society pages.

If you live someplace where a lot of other people don't, it may be relatively easy to deal with the newspaper. Merely call up the lifestyle editor and ask about the fee, deadline, and requirements. Sometimes a standard form exists; if not, fill out the information yourself. Perhaps you're from an intact nuclear family, this is your first marriage, and both your parents are alive? In that case, you simply type on a piece of 8½″ x 11″ white paper that Mr. and Mrs. Your Father's Name of Your Street Address announce the engagement of their daughter, Your Name, to Your Fiancé's Name, the son of His Parents' Names, of Wherever He's From. And you tell them the month the wedding is planned. Put your name, address, and phone number in the upper right corner and put the whole thing in the mail, or drop it by the newspaper office, perhaps with a black-and-white glossy photograph showing you at your best (which usually means in a string of pearls). After that, sit back and wait.

However, if you find yourself in an urban center, things become a bit dicier. Lots of people live there, and a lot of them are getting married. Space is at a premium. The laws of supply and demand take over and the principles of competition apply. If this is your situation—if you're in a city where it's just not that simple to get into the paper—don't give up. Carefully study your newspaper's society page to divine any hidden agenda underlying its editorial policy, and then give them exactly what they really want.

Close examination of *The New York Times* is good training for approaching any newspaper in any major market. Brides who crack the "Women's Sports Pages" as they're sometimes called (alternatively: "Mergers & Acquisitions") have the knack of furnishing the information that earns them a spot. How do they do it? There seem to be two basic strategies: (a) be of a humble background and become a brain surgeon or run the mayor's office; and (b) be of a grand background. You're more apt to be seen by thousands of Sunday brunchers with ink on their fingers if your last novel was a giant best-seller, the groom is a major basketball star, and/or if your grandfather invented the aerosol can or silicon chip or some other technology that altered the course of civilization. Failing that, it's still impressive, never passé, to have the same last name as, and direct lineage to, a signer of the Declaration of Independence or a President of the United States.

Keep all this in mind as you proceed with your engagement announcement, and again later when you supply your wedding announcement (in New York, at least three weeks before the ceremony). Of course, you could always just content yourself with the Passages section of *People* magazine, but even there, frankly, it helps to be a member of the Rolling Stones. As for the leading out-of-town papers:

ATLANTA JOURNAL-CONSTITUTION, Box 4689, Atlanta, GA 30302 (404) 526-5415. They won't announce your engagement, only your wedding. Just call the direct dial listed here and ask the person who answers to send you the form. If you send a photo too, it should be only of the bride's face. Your announcement will be printed as long as they have the information at least ten days prior to the ceremony. No fee.

BOSTON GLOBE, 135 Morrissey Boulevard, Boston, MA 02107 (617) 929-2000. Send the names of the couple and where they're from, the names of the couple's parents and where they're from, the proposed date and site of the wedding, and a daytime phone number to Society Editor. Make sure it all arrives at least two months before the wedding; nothing afterward. They say they print everything that's not late. No fee.

CHICAGO TRIBUNE, Tribune Tower, 435 North Michigan Avenue, Chicago, IL 60611. To try for what they call "editorial consideration," call Tempo/Women/Weddings (312) 222-4049 and listen to the recording (they won't talk to you directly); then, at least three weeks before the ceremony, send them the requested information along with two daytime phone numbers and a stamped, self-addressed envelope if you want your photo returned if you don't get in. If you don't hear from them within one week, assume you haven't. (At that point you can elect to pay a fee: phone Suzanne Alton at (312) 222-3232 and she'll send you a form. Without a photo the fee is $49; with a photo it's $98. You pay twice if you announce both your engagement and your wedding.)

LOS ANGELES TIMES, Times Mirror Square, Los Angeles, CA 90053 (213) 237-7000. Write to Evie de Wolfe, View Section/Society for the form. It's interactive: you circle things (Bride-Elect or Bride; Fiancé or Bridegroom); check off boxes

Los Angeles Times

(CIRCLE ONE)
BRIDE-ELECT:
BRIDE:_____

(CIRCLE ONE)
FIANCE:
BRIDEGROOM:_____

ADDRESS_____

ADDRESS_____

PHONE_____

PHONE_____

SCHOOLS_____ ☐ ATTENDED ☐ GRADUATED

SCHOOLS_____ ☐ ATTENDED ☐ GRADUATED

_____ ☐ ATTENDED ☐ GRADUATED

_____ ☐ ATTENDED ☐ GRADUATED

BUSINESS AND OTHER AFFILIATIONS_____

BUSINESS AND OTHER AFFILIATIONS_____

FATHER:_____

FATHER:_____

ADDRESS_____

ADDRESS_____

CITY   STATE   ZIP

CITY   STATE   ZIP

PHONE_____

PHONE_____

FATHER'S OCCUPATION/AFFILIATIONS_____

FATHER'S OCCUPATION/AFFILIATIONS_____

TITLE/FIRM_____

TITLE/FIRM_____

MOTHER:_____

MOTHER:_____

ADDRESS_____

ADDRESS_____

CITY   STATE   ZIP

CITY   STATE   ZIP

PHONE_____

PHONE_____

MOTHER'S OCCUPATION/AFFILIATIONS:

MOTHER'S OCCUPATION/AFFILIATIONS:_____

TITLE/FIRM_____

TITLE/FIRM_____

ENGAGEMENT INFORMATION

DATE AND PLACE OF ANNOUNCEMENT_____ WEDDING DATE_____

WEDDING INFORMATION

DATE_____HOUR_____ ☐ AM ☐ PM   PLACE AND CITY _____

RECEPTION AT_____

QUESTIONNAIRE COURTESY *LOS ANGELES TIMES*

51

Dial (212) 556-7325 for the tape recording of instructions you'll have to listen to more than once, they come at you so fast. Jot down as many of the directions as you possibly can; then hit the redial button, start the tape again, and jot down some more. *Au fond*, you must:

• Type your announcement clearly.
• Give them names, addresses, and occupations for all four parents, living and dead.
• Tell the schools, ages, and accomplishments of you and your fiancé.
• Furnish the day and date of your wedding.
• Mention previous marriages of either the bride or groom and how they ended.
• Supply four daytime and two nighttime phone numbers in case they need to reach you.
• Give them an optional 5″ x 7″ or 8″ x 10″ black-and-white glossy photo (the new kind showing both the bride and groom, with heads at equal level, is probably preferable—your brother can take it and you can be wearing shorts at the time, as it must be cropped such that you're seen only from the waist up).
• Understand there's no fee and no guarantee.

Send your package to: Society Editor, The New York Times, 229 West 43rd Street, New York, NY 10036 as early as possible. Don't quibble and don't be witty. Don't say a previous marriage ended badly. Don't question what the point of giving a dead person's address might be. Do, however, consider the intriguing off-the-society-page ploy sometimes used by couples in the same high-visibility industry: announce your engagement in *another* section! In the Media column, say. Or as a feature in Arts and Leisure, or Business Day. Ask your publicist to take care of it.

(Attended or Graduated); fill out phone numbers and addresses. A bulleted summary of directions capitalizes and sets in bold certain points of emphasis:

• All information must be COMPLETE, BRIEF, and LEGIBLE. PRINT all names in full with addresses. If parents are divorced or deceased, please state.
• At least one of the engaged or bridal pair MUST HAVE LOCAL TIES.
• ENGAGEMENT information must be received AT LEAST 3 MONTHS before wedding date.

The *Times* does not charge for publishing engagement or wedding announcements. Neither does it guarantee that any story submitted to its editorial department will be published. However, all submissions will be given every chance for inclusion either in the View Section or in the *Times*'s suburban editions. *Please submit one form only.*

WASHINGTON POST, 1150 15th Street NW, Washington, DC 20071 (202) 334-6000. *Step One.* The operator puts you through to the Bridal Desk and you get a tape on which you're told not to be discouraged, your call will be returned. *Step Two.* It is. What's more, you are sent a form telling you all about the required information and the deadline you must observe. Engagement and wedding announcements appear in the Wednesday edition (in most other newspapers, it's Sunday). There is a fee, figured by the line (your photo, should you elect to include one, is paid by the line as well). The fee is subject to change, but expect around $11.50 per line; there are 14 lines to a column inch.

What are your parents going through now that you've announced your engagement? Berkeley, California, psychotherapist Karen Faircloth weighs the emotional baggage and offers advice on dealing with the people you loved first.

Dear Therapist Karen:

My mother is driving me crazy. My wedding is still two months away, but she can't stop calling me at work about my dress, the place cards, my future mother-in-law. You'd think she was the one getting married! Meanwhile, my father seems to be working late hours at his office—he isn't really around that much. What do you make of all this?

Loving Daughter

Dear Loving Daughter:

We know it's not their first wedding—presumably, they've had at least their own—but it seems your parents are having a lot of anxiety. Your mother is acting out with her interference. And your father is acting out *his* underlying anxiety by denying he has it: he has just disappeared. Does any of this feel familiar to you? Did your parents act this way around any other life-crisis events? How were they when you were waiting for your college acceptances? Marriage—especially their daughter's—is a life-crisis event, so why should they be any different this time? Don't let them transfer their anxiety to you, though; perhaps you can remember how you've handled them in the past.

Good luck!
Karen

NOT-SO-MODERN BRIDE

An ancient code continues to dictate much of the contemporary wedding. The canny bride adapts to it without offending her blended and reblended family, the corporate culture, her gender politics. How? She simply chooses wisely whenever confronted with a difficult situation. Try your hand at these potential vignettes. Answers at the bottom.

1 You have been living together ever since that summer at the Loeb when you stage-managed *Julius Caesar* and he appeared in modern dress. To become engaged, he insists upon a dowry. You . . .
   (a) tell him to get lost
   (b) present him with the bananas, earthenware pots, and bird-of-paradise plumes traditional to ancient New Guinea
   (c) remind him that you have a B.A. from Stanford, an anchor position on the network news, and your first husband will continue child-support payments

2 The senior partners are coming to the wedding. At the reception, they should be seated . . .
   (a) at a table by themselves so they can talk about which of the middle managers should be fired this week
   (b) with your sorority sisters so they can talk about things they shouldn't
   (c) with some other senior partners so they can do a deal

3 Your groom's mother's second husband ran off with her first husband's sister, with the result that today a lot of people aren't speaking to one another. But your groom, the child of his mother's first marriage, is very fond of his cousin, the child of his aunt and ex-stepfather. To make everyone happy, you should . . .
   (a) elope
   (b) write about it for episodic TV
   (c) invite all concerned to the wedding, seating your in-laws' home-wrecking relations at a table in the corner and inviting your groom's cousin to be a flower girl

4 At a shower, the guests wonder whether there were any powerful alliances created by marriage in the twentieth century. You say yes and cite the past and pending marriages of . . .
   (a) Jane Fonda to Roger Vadim
   (b) Jane Fonda to Tom Hayden
   (c) Jane Fonda to Ted Turner

5 You are pressed by the same group to name two twentieth-century

American fathers whose fortunes could only improve when their children joined in marriage. Easy, you say. And point to . . .

(a) dime-store founder F. W. Woolworth and financier E. F. Hutton
(b) Governor Mario Cuomo and (the memory of) Senator Robert F. Kennedy
(c) junk-bond king Saul Steinberg and media baron Laurence Tisch

Answers: All are perfectly correct except 2(a).

Putting It All in Perspective 1

56 *As you join humanity's long and relentless trip to the altar, think about this:*

- The word "wife" originally meant "woman," but the word "husband" originally meant "master of the house."
- Cicero said, "The first bond of society is marriage."
- Purification by earth, fire, or water has been practiced by numerous cultures throughout history. Just before the wedding, the bride may be submerged in water (a Jewish bride today may still visit "the mikvah lady"), or fumigated with incense, or have her body smeared with mud or paint.
- Marriage by capture was legal in England as late as the thirteenth century.
- When the English settled in Jamestown, the price of a new bride there was 120 pounds of tobacco.
- In Arab countries, the bride-price is sometimes as much as one-third her father's annual income.

• Among the Gisu of East Africa, the bride-price was paid in rats, chickens, goats, and cattle. Six goats equaled one cow.

• A Pennsylvania Dutch girl of the eighteenth or nineteenth century might spend her adolescence stitching a dozen quilts. When she finished, she would announce her readiness for a husband, and begin work on a thirteenth quilt, the Wedding Quilt.

• Brides are still for sale in parts of New Guinea.

• It wasn't until 1879 that the Supreme Court of the United States outlawed polygamy.

• The longest engagement on record is sixty-seven years. Adriana Martinez and Octavio Guillen had both turned eighty-two by the time they married in June 1969.

• The Cullinan diamond, discovered in 1905, was twice as big as any diamond yet found. It was cut, in Amsterdam, on February 10, 1908, at precisely 2:45 P.M. At 2:46 the diamond cutter fainted.

• Napoleon and Josephine signed separate documents, in 1801, specifying Josephine's dowry of 12,000 francs and Napoleon's responsibilities toward their future estate . . . an early version of a prenuptial agreement.

• A bride and groom in New York, in 1990, were so determined to divide future expenses equally that their prenuptial contract stipulated splitting the then three-dollar toll on the George Washington Bridge.

• The invitation to the wedding of English rock star Rod Stewart to model Rachel Hunter, in 1990, asked guests to witness the marriage vows at a ceremony in Beverly Hills, followed by a "Reception and Piss-up" at the Four Seasons Hotel. "Piss-up" is a British phrase having to do with drinking.

• Cracker Jill: In some parts of the South an old custom is still observed at the bridesmaids' prewedding luncheon for the bride, her attendants, and the mothers. A cake, with pink sugar frosting, has been baked with charms: a heart for love, a dime for wealth, an anchor for hope, a ring for marriage. Sometimes the charms inside the cake are attached to ribbons streaming from it; sometimes they are revealed only with the eating. Whichever the case, it is believed that the guest who gets the ring will be the next to wed.

ALWAYS
A BRIDE

REALIZING

YOUR

DEEPEST

WISHES

he bridal fantasy, with its origins in passivity and competitiveness, is nevertheless an expression of individuality and fulfillment. In full flower, its elments combine to create a bride whose regal presence charms the pants off everyone in the hall. England's Princess Diana ("being a princess is like being a bride every day of your life") is the chief role model. But the attributes she embodies really don't have to be articulated to most brides, who have understood since girlhood that living a myth is a matter of analyzing its components. Being a bride has nothing to do with brilliance or accomplishment or diligence—it has to do with being specially blessed. Only certain traits matter. And if you know what they are, they come as naturally as wearing silk and satin and trailing a long train.

SERENITY. Whatever it takes, throughout civilization brides have maintained the unruffled, unflappable, somewhat aloof air that comes as a result of total security and dominion over all. Does the bride offer tiny gloved waves as the limo pulls up to the curb? Good, because her ability to communicate imperviousness to the madding throng actually reassures it: the crowd understands that at least there's one special someone who will always remain cool in the crisis of their own chaotic impulses. (And that the photographer can't ruin this party before it starts, no matter how long he takes with the official pictures.)

SUPREMACY. Brides simply must insist on ruling. Otherwise, it's hard to justify being the center of attention. A bride is not necessarily spoiled, however—and she never throws a fit, even at her sister, who is balking at wearing her special maid-of-honor dress just because the bustle makes her look fat. The bride uses a winning smile and soft gesture to get her way. And does.

BELOVEDNESS. Because it's good for everybody if the bride is adored by all who meet her, she conducts herself according to standards of sweetness, solicitude, and discretion that anyone else would find impossible to maintain. She makes self-effacing wisecracks with her groom's old girlfriend, personally inquires after the state of Uncle Herman's gallbladder, and seems oblivious to the empty meeting hall downstairs at the hotel, which the ushers have dubbed the Marijuana Room.

THINNESS. Because a bride is in a beautiful dress; because she is in pictures, and on the tape; because she may soon be pregnant and huge, she is always thin. If she didn't start that way, she gets that way. Perhaps she goes to Weight Watchers and drops twenty-five pounds. Perhaps she goes overboard, verging on anorexia. Perhaps she's only thin*ner*. But she floats down the aisle, lighter than air. And hungrier than hell.

FLIRTATIOUSNESS. If on this day above all others it's obvious to whom her affections belong, it's also safe to flirt. The

WHAT TO DO WITH YOUR TIARA

Wear it by day. Put it on your bedpost at night.

bride may lower her eyes demurely when the Best Man compliments her, thus telegraphing that things might have been different were it not that life takes such strange turns. The bride's favors are so powerful that such behavior will not only send the Best Man (and Grandfather, should she try it on him) into paroxysms, but also give everyone something juicy to gossip about later.

GENUINENESS. Way down deep, the bride is of the people. As a result of their own needs and yearnings, and via tortuous convolutions, they have made her who she is today. She understands that. Naturally it would be undignified to slum, but still, these folks are in some sense her family, and their concerns will always be hers. It's to her credit that she has such great heart and vast resources of empathy that she's on the floor even now, shimmying under the limbo stick.

BEAUTY. A bride is breathtaking. Her hair shines, her skin glows, her teeth gleam, her figure excites. So what if her face wouldn't exactly launch a thousand ships? At least they could use her lantern jaw as a beacon.

EFFERVESCENCE. Perhaps a bride stops short of giggling, perhaps she doesn't—but she definitely has a good time. She may also have a cold, a tension headache, a raging fever, but no one would ever know. She's like the champagne—light and bubbly. She smiles, laughs, chats, and is thoroughly spontaneous. This party is so much fun and it's so wonderful to see everyone! Hi, Uncle Herman!

VIRGINITY. A bride has never been touched except innocently. She may enjoy proving this by getting one of her friends from medical school to write out a statement and sign it with someone's name. Or she may bag that and think of her virginity metaphorically: if the truth is she has slept with half the city of Dallas, not to mention her groom—she's still never before been touched by marriage.

SEVEN SUPERSTITIONS

1 A bride must not be completely dressed until the moment she sets out for the church. At that time a final stitch should be added to her dress for good luck.

2 It's bad luck not to burn the bride's bouquet within one month of her wedding.

3 It's bad luck to drop the ring during the ceremony.

4 It's good luck for the bride to be kissed by a chimney sweep on her wedding day.

5 It's good luck for a bride to carry a handkerchief—because

if she cries on her wedding day, her marriage will never make her cry again.

6 It's good luck for the bride to wear or carry "something old, something new, something borrowed, something blue."

7 It's good luck for the bride to slip a coin into her shoe as a token of her groom's love.

To make sure the bride is kissed by a chimney sweep on her wedding day, hire one.

ATLANTA
CHIMNEY SWEEP
(404) 981-8836

· · · · · · · · · · ·

DENVER
ASH EATERS
CHIMNEY SWEEPS
(303) 699-6678

· · · · · · · · · · ·

ST. LOUIS
CHIMNEY SWEEP LTD.
(314) 966-7205

SAN ANTONIO
ABLE CHIMNEY SWEEP
(512) 497-4416

· · · · · · · · · · ·

SAN FRANCISCO
THE CHIMNEY SWEEP
(415) 239-1446

· · · · · · · · · · ·

SEATTLE
CHIM CHIMMANEY
CHIMNEY SWEEP
(206) 745-0320

THIRTY-TWO FANTASY BRIDES WHO WEREN'T EVEN REAL

1. Jeanette MacDonald in *The Love Parade*, 1929
2. Marlene Dietrich in *The Blue Angel*, 1930
3. Claudette Colbert in *It Happened One Night*, 1934
4. Vivien Leigh in *Gone With the Wind*, 1939
5. Katharine Hepburn in *The Philadelphia Story*, 1940
6. Katharine Hepburn in *Woman of the Year*, 1942
7. Cathy O'Donnell in *The Best Years of Our Lives*, 1946
8. Elizabeth Taylor in *Father of the Bride*, 1950
9. Doris Day in *By the Light of the Silvery Moon*, 1953
10. Jane Powell in *Seven Brides for Seven Brothers*, 1954
11. Debbie Reynolds in *The Catered Affair*, 1956
12. Grace Kelly in *High Society*, 1956
13. Audrey Hepburn in *Funny Face*, 1957
14. Julie Andrews in *The Sound of Music*, 1965
15. Katharine Ross in *The Graduate*, 1967
16. Jeanne Moreau in *The Bride Wore Black*, 1968
17. Ali MacGraw in *Love Story*, 1970
18. Rosalind Harris in *Fiddler on the Roof*, 1971
19. Talia Shire in *The Godfather*, 1972
20. Barbra Streisand in *A Star Is Born*, 1976
21. Amy Stryker in *A Wedding*, 1978
22. Beverly D'Angelo in *Hair*, 1979
23. Talia Shire in *Rocky II*, 1979
24. Amy Madigan in *Twice in a Lifetime*, 1985
25. Meryl Streep in *Heartburn*, 1986
26. Isabella Rossellini in *Cousins*, 1989
27. Annabella Sciorra in *True Love*, 1989
28. Julia Roberts in *Steel Magnolias*, 1990
29. Molly Ringwald in *Betsy's Wedding*, 1990
30. Laura San Giacomo in *Once Around*, 1991
31. Emily Lloyd in *Scorchers*, 1991
32. Kim Basinger in *The Marrying Man*, 1991

HAS THE WOMAN IN THE PHOTO BEEN ENGAGED EIGHT TIMES? PERHAPS NOT, BUT THERE ARE SEVERAL FAMOUS BRIDES WHO MARRIED MORE THAN ONCE

TIMOTHY LEE

Alphabetical by last name; asterisk denotes three or more times

INGRID BERGMAN *
AGATHA CHRISTIE
CHER
BETTE DAVIS *
KITTY DUKAKIS
NORA EPHRON *
JANE FONDA *
BETTY FORD
EVA GABOR *
ZSA ZSA GABOR *
JUDY GARLAND *
WHOOPI GOLDBERG
JANET LEIGH *

ALI MACGRAW *
MADONNA
LIZA MINNELLI
YOKO ONO *
JACQUELINE ONASSIS
DIANA ROSS
ELIZABETH TAYLOR *
CHERYL TIEGS *
GLORIA VANDERBILT *
BARBARA WALTERS
MARTHA WASHINGTON
TAMMY WYNETTE *

No bride can be expected to know everything all the time, but that's all right—some things she can look up, or read about in magazines. Try the printed matter below. What isn't a resource is a diversion.

Magazines

BRIDAL GUIDE Its distinguishing feature: special pages printed on heavy stock that can serve as planners and checklists for every aspect of the wedding. You can rip these pages out of the magazine and save them.

BRIDE'S The just-married mother of all bridal journalism, it has a whopping 4 million readers per issue and so much advertising that its weight is comparable to the average phone book's. Do you read it for the service pieces, the way *Playboy*'s subscribers read that magazine for the fiction? Maybe, but you're probably studying the gowns in all those ads, too.

ELEGANT BRIDE The new one. It costs $4.95, like *Bride's*, instead of $4.50, like *Modern Bride*.

MODERN BRIDE They say *Modern Bride* isn't quite as successful as *Bride's*, but the truth is, it's hard to tell the difference between the two. Another slick showcase for advertisers.

How-to Books

AFFORDABLE WEDDINGS, by Leta W. Clark (Fireside/Simon & Schuster, $10.95). Chiefly a crafts resource, this is for the bride who wants a beautiful wedding on a budget. There are patterns and directions for making everything from the cake the stripper jumps out of at the bachelor dinner to a patchwork huppah for the ceremony.

BIG WEDDINGS ON A SMALL BUDGET, by Diane Warner (Writer's Digest Books, $12.95). How to get the price of a wedding for 300 people down to as little as half or 20 percent of the average cost. Suggestions include purchasing the food for the reception from a wholesale food supplier and becoming your own caterer; also, renting the bride's dress, renting the reception site, renting a top-quality camera and taking your own pictures.

THE MESSAGE OF MARRIAGE, by Kristina Garvin (Weatherford Publications, $8.95). Want to learn how to word it on the invitation when your mother is a judge and your father isn't? How to let people know that you and your groom will be hyphenating your name after your marriage? How to select an appropriate "ensemble"? If so, get this book. It tells everything about wedding stationery—even how to mail printed cards when it's necessary to postpone the wedding or recall the invitations should illness, accident, or change of heart strike. *To order, write 6447 Loma de Cristo, El Paso, TX 79912, or phone (915) 585-0228.*

PLACES, by Hannelore Hahn and Tatiana Stoumen. A directory of public places for private events and private places for public events. How to select the perfect nontraditional site for your wedding: 200 listings (and 400 photos) for Boston, Philadelphia, Washington, Atlanta, Dallas/Houston, New Orleans, Chicago, Los Angeles, and San Francisco. *To order, send $24.95 (postpaid) to Places, 810 Gracie Station, New York, NY 10028.*

THE TIFFANY WEDDING, by John Loring, with an introduction by Patricia Warner (Doubleday, $50.00). A sumptuous presentation of the wedding as part of the good life. Lush full-color photos of Tiffany merchandise in pretty settings are juxtaposed with instructions on how to give a small prenuptial contract-signing luncheon for your intended, his lawyer, and your lawyer; how to announce your engagement, presuming one father is a bank president and the other founded a brokerage firm; how to cover your swimming pool to make a dance floor; how to give your first dinner as a newlywed ("If you burn the soup, whip out that standby jar of caviar"). Completely silly, but a lot of fun to look at.

WEDDINGS, by Martha Stewart (Crown, $60.00). The lavish, oversized, full-color wish book crammed with photos and ideas. If you can't afford to buy a copy—or if it's so heavy you can't carry it—go to the library and take notes. The woman is a wonder.

Inspirational Books

THE NEW JEWISH WEDDING, by Anita Diamant (Summit, $9.95). Indispensable. History, inspiration, and a planner too.

THE OXFORD BOOK OF MARRIAGE, edited by Helge Rubinstein (Oxford University Press, $19.95). From prose and poetry, favorite passages about weddings and marriage.

WEDDING READINGS, by Eleanor Munro (Viking, $17.95). Centuries of writing and rituals for love and marriage, selected with a sharp ear for the lyrical. A great gift.

Etiquette Books

DEAR ABBY ON PLANNING YOUR WEDDING, by Abigail Van Buren (Andrews & McMeel, $8.95). In letters-to-Abby format, an updating of social conventions and rules of etiquette.

MISS MANNERS' GUIDE FOR THE TURN OF THE MILLENNIUM, by Judith Martin (Fireside/Simon & Schuster, $15.95). Advice from the columnist, who answers letters querying etiquette in various areas. About weddings: what to do if the bride is pregnant; how to have a shipboard wedding; more. Includes counsel on attendants' duties, the invitation, the guest list, menus.

SHOWERS, by Beverly Clark (Wilshire Publications, $8.95). A complete guide to hosting a bridal shower, with special attention to the second-time bride.

YOU AND YOUR WEDDING, by Winifred Gray (Bantam, $4.95). A handbook with one million copies in print over the past twenty-five years. It's hard to read, has no illustrations, and seems dated—but it does include everything from how to phrase the invitation and word the ceremony to a recipe for a broccoli ring.

Planners

BRIDE'S WEDDING PLANNER, by the Editors of *Bride's* magazine (Fawcett, $9.95). A timetable with insider tips, reader worksheets, and comments about everything from bone china to the contraceptive sponge.

CHECK LIST FOR A PERFECT WEDDING, by Barbara Lee Follet (Doubleday, $4.95). Pocket-size and compact, so it's ideal to carry with you on your errands. One million brides have used it since the original edition in 1961.

EMILY POST'S WEDDING PLANNER, by Elizabeth L. Post (Harper Perennial, $4.95). Simple, tasteful. Like white bread, or just the upper crust. (To do during the Last Month: "See about a floater insurance policy to cover your gifts. . . .")

GOBLE & SHEA'S COMPLETE WEDDING PLAN-NER (Questar, $10.00). The usual guidelines, checklists, and diagrams—with a twist: the authors are mother and daughter.
THE WEDDING PLANNER, by Martha Stewart (Clarkson Potter, $35.00). Yes! Other planners are paperbacks for under fifteen dollars; Martha's is a robin's-egg-blue leatherette comb-bound tabbed organizer in a full-color gift slipcase for more than twice as much. Oh well. Get it if you possibly can. It has color photos throughout, and hints, and recipes. And on the slipcase? Not just a picture of Martha in wedding finery but also a picture of Martha on a cellular phone at what appears to be base camp for the caterers.
THE WORKING WOMAN'S WEDDING PLANNER, by Susan Tasui-D'Arcy (Prentice Hall, Inc., $14.95). For that matter, you could use it if you were unemployed. Seems pretty expensive for what it is—the usual countdown motif.

Memories and Memoir

THE BRIDESMAIDS, by Judith Balaban Quine (Pocket Books, $5.95). The *New York Times* best-seller about Grace Kelly's wedding and how everyone dealt with living happily ever after. Spirited writing, great reading, and neat details (the future Serene Highness bought the little white socks and Mary Janes for her four flower girls from the J. C. Penney catalogue; upon hearing loud explosions from a fireworks display for the bride and groom, King Farouk of Egypt thought he was under attack and ducked for cover; had Princess Grace ever wished to divorce, she would not have been permitted to keep her children; more). The best—give all your bridesmaids a copy.
WEDDING MEMORIES, by Beverly Clark (Wilshire Publications, $16.95). So you can write down who the guests were and who the President was the day you were married. Illuminated blank pages, like a baby's record book.

deally, the bridal couple's attendants complement them perfectly, making them appear always more handsome and blessed as a duo. This takes work, and for that reason it is wise to give some thought to the selection of the wedding party. Bridesmaids and groomsmen have time-honored roles to play. They're there to support you, just as they were in the time of marriage by capture. Back then, all the girls dressed alike in an effort to confuse the marauding boys from the other tribe. The bride's friends protected her; the groom's friends helped him— and whether individual groomsmen and maids got together afterward for a drink of their own is lost to history. The most competent attendants are chosen according to certain traits of character, but if you don't have friends who possess these qualities, grab whomever you can get. Being in someone's wedding is a pretty thankless job.

STAMINA. This prerequisite is especially pertinent when large quantities of alcohol have been consumed the night before the small but essential breakfast hosted by the mother of the bride. Stamina is also crucial during lengthy religious ceremonies, while dancing with Uncle Herman, and at the airport when the flight back to St. Louis is delayed eight hours.

CHEERFULNESS. Don't take this personally, but some portions of your wedding (the receiving line leaps to mind) are apt to be tedious, not to mention hard on the feet. This is when the unflaggingly perky types carry the day and the good sport is all-important.

INDEPENDENTLY BANKROLLED. You're asking a friend to buy a dress and shoe combination that's probably unwearable in the real world, or to buy or rent a tux. You're also asking this friend to pay for some or all of the following: a party for you, shower presents, a wedding present, an airline ticket, a hotel room, a rental car, something to wear to the rehearsal dinner. Hey —it's an honor. (*Note:* Some experts say the bride should pay for the accommodations for out-of-town attendants.)

VETERAN OF OTHER WEDDINGS. The value of a person who more or less knows the drill, and can get into it, is incalcula-

What Does the Bride Give to Her Attendants?

For centuries, gloves. But the current faves are a necklace, a locket, a bracelet, a picture frame, a decorative clock, a perfume bottle, a mirror, a vanity jar, a letter opener, a bud vase, earrings, a scarf, a compact.

What Does the Groom Give to His Men?

A key ring, a belt buckle, a silk tie, a pewter mug, a wallet, a pen and pencil set, cuff links; a lot to drink.

ble. Does the candidate have toasts, verse, song at his ready command? Has she perfected an unself-conscious gait for coming down the aisle? Can he loosen up everyone in the limo? Does she know how to do the hora? Will he take the gifts people brought to the reception back to the house? Tie old shoes to the getaway car? Dance with the maid of honor? Your grandmother?

HAS ALWAYS THOUGHT YOU WERE REALLY SPE-CIAL. Exceptional candidates are often found among sorority sisters and fraternity brothers, or real sisters and real brothers— halves and steps included. The person you went to kindergarten with is also a nice touch, as well as your old best friend who moved to the other coast and your mentor from the office. As for people you're less sure of? You probably really should consider the groom's siblings. His offspring is another question.

Additional desirable trait in a bridesmaid:
Loves dyed shoes in any color, even bubble gum.

Additional desirable traits in an usher:
Has tendency toward mild horseplay (as echo of marriage by capture); gives good toasts; can tell left from right (for seating duties); has driver's license (for getaway car).

Can the Best Man Be a Woman and the Maid of Honor a Man?

Certainly. That's the format when the best friends of both the bride and groom are people of the opposite sex. Anyway, it has happened.

STANDING OUT AT
BLENDING IN

The Bridesmaid

The bridesmaid, who has accepted the invitation to spend a fair portion of her salary on attending you, is clearly committed to doing a good job. Remembering that the job in question is simply to give you cover, and that this is your big day, not hers, she may nevertheless excel if she observes these simple pointers:

Do find a subtle way to compliment the bride on her obvious and extraordinary sexiness. Giving her tassles at the lingerie shower gets the point across.

Do take emergency supplies—needle, thread, aspirin, extra jewelry—to the bridal room, and be prepared to minister to others. (At her wedding no less than Princess Grace borrowed a pair of diamond and pearl earrings, from bridesmaid Judith Balaban.)

Do point the blossoms of your bouquet at the congregation, not your stomach. Who wants to look at a bunch of stems?

Do bow during the prayers.

Do stay on your diet long enough to fit into your dress. You can eat all you want at the reception.

Do everything you must to catch the bridal bouquet. Illegal basketball moves are perfectly acceptable.

Don't balk when it turns out all the bridesmaids have to wear Dynel hair swatches. (And *don't* giggle when you hear people trying to sort out their confusion as you come down the aisle: "She has such beautiful, long, blond hair." "And *she* has such beautiful, long, red hair." "And she has such beautiful, long, *black* hair." "And she . . .")

Don't affect that queer, hitching gait for the walk down the aisle unless it's specifically requested and everyone else is doing it too.

Don't lock your knees during the ceremony.

Don't chew gum.

Don't look bored.

Don't ignore Uncle Herman.

Don't be mean to the ushers.

Don't forget to give a present to the bride and groom.

The maid or matron of honor has even more official duties. In addition to going to all the parties, helping the bride get dressed, and just generally setting the tone for the rest of the bridesmaids, she is supposed to sign the marriage license, precede the bride and her father in the procession, arrange the bride's train and veil during the ceremony (and hold the groom's ring, if there is one), lift the bride's veil for the kiss, stand next to the groom in the receiving line, and sit on his left at the bride's table. Probably, she also went out to Kleinfeld's with the bride and helped her choose her dress.

PHOTO COURTESY JIM HJELM/A PRIVATE COLLECTION

CONFESSIONS OF A FLOWER GIRL

Flower girls are usually (but not always—rules are there to be broken) under the age of nine. They carry flowers. They like dressing up and having fun. They don't like getting nervous.

Claire Heffernan, age eleven, who carried a needlepoint hoop with ribbons and white roses at her big sister's wedding, remembers realizing just as she was starting down the aisle that unlike the way it had been at the rehearsal, there were now people in the pews. "I was kind of scared," she admits. "Everyone was looking. My knees shook. I was afraid I'd get separated from my little sister."

And indeed, Kate Heffernan, age nine, who is Claire's sister and preceded her in the procession, recalls suddenly wondering whether she was walking too fast; she very much wanted to turn around and see if Claire was still there. In Kate's opinion it took "a minute" to get down the aisle; Claire thinks it was longer.

Both girls wore teal velvet dresses with white gloves, and at the reception everyone told them they looked really pretty. Claire thought the most fun of the whole wedding was when the bride was putting on her

PHOTO COURTESY BRIDAL ORIGINALS

going-away outfit at the hotel and the groom was getting dressed in the room next door; all the attendants ran back and forth "and yelled jokes at each other." Kate says she would definitely be a flower girl again, if asked. Her advice to other flower girls: "It's fun. Don't be nervous. It goes by really fast."

THE BEST MAN

In addition to mingling with the guests and being able to direct people to the parking lot or rest room, there are a few extra responsibilities that fall to the best man:

• At the rehearsal, brief the ushers about special seating ar-

rangements and guests to watch for.
• Sign the marriage license.
• Make sure you have a check available for the officiant's fee (give it to him just before or after the ceremony).
• Accompany the groom to the ceremony.
• Enter the vestibule after the groom during the procession; then stand behind the groom, slightly to the left.
• Hold the bride's ring, even if there is a ring bearer (his is fake).
• Play big brother to the ring bearer.
• Walk with the maid of honor after the ceremony.
• Drive the bridal couple to the reception (unless a limo's been hired).
• Propose the first toast to the new couple; collect and read any telegrams.
• Take charge of the honeymoon luggage; make sure the groom has the tickets and reservations he needs for the honeymoon.

PHOTO COURTESY AFTER SIX

LYDIA MAY STUDIOS, CAMBRIDGE, MASSACHUSETTS

Oh sure, the guy you're marrying is a regular he-man. He'll have to be to shoulder all this:

TRADITIONAL RESPONSIBILITIES

- Select engagement ring for bride
- Go shopping with bride
- Have blood test
- Plan affordable honeymoon
- Get marriage license (with bride)
- Talk to clergyperson (with bride)
- Pay for bride's bouquet, mothers' corsages, ushers' and fathers' boutonnieres
- Give bride gift
- Give ushers gifts
- Get haircut

NEW, TRENDIER RESPONSIBILITIES

- Select rings with bride
- Agree to wear wedding band (*Note:* 90 percent of all grooms are currently doing this.)
- Address invitations in calligraphic hand
- Maintain RSVP data base on computer
- Drop ex-wife civil note
- Be civil to bride's ex-husband
- Take bride's son to circus
- Pose for engagement and wedding photos
- Attend embarrassing theme shower
- Search New Age literature for inspiring vows
- Attend sports event with ushers
- Take your mother to lunch
- Make sure you look okay
- Split cost of everything with bride

SEEING THE BIG PICTURE

Hiring a Wedding Consultant

Wedding consultants

Kelly Gladder *Annena Sorenson* *Robbi Ernst* *Kristina Garvin*

he wedding consultant is hot. In fact, in 1989 her business was ranked the nineteenth most rapidly growing in the country. With the average cost of the American wedding currently at somewhere between $14,000 and $15,000, it's easy to see why; no one wants to make a costly mistake. Responsibility once left to the bride's family is now shouldered by a trained professional who can negotiate prices, keep costs down, check on details, and help with hand-holding, decision making, and stage directing. The wedding consultant will save steps by gathering the invitation samples, the floral albums, the cassettes of musicians. She'll take the worry out of rehearsals, and on the wedding day she is the point person, helping the bride to dress, cuing the attendants, overseeing the schedule. In the long run, she will almost certainly save you time and money and prevent stress or even disaster. Find her early. Work with her. Pay her. But re-

PHOTO OF KRISTINA GARVIN BY MICHAEL'S STUDIO, PETALUMA, CALIFORNIA

PHOTO OF ROBBI ERNST BY BACHRACH PHOTOGRAPHERS, SAN FRANCISCO

PHOTO OF KELLY GLADDER AND ANNENA SORENSON BY CINDY GILMORE OF LIFESTYLE PHOTOGRAPHY, PALO ALTO, CALIFORNIA

member that while wedding consultants can be certified, they're not regulated. Don't put up with:

CONFLICT OF INTEREST. The new wedding consultant is likely to be in business for herself, rather than working for the bridal registry at your department store. She should be able to give you several choices of sites, menus, floral packages, musicians, bakers, caterers, and she should probably be able to book a block of reduced-rate hotel rooms and make low-fare group travel arrangements for your guests. Usually, she can find discounts for you—after all, she goes back to the same suppliers over and over. But be wary if she's taking commissions. In the bad old days this practice was customary, and some still do it; unfortunately, it tends to take the art of the kickback to real lows. Most reputable wedding planners are certified by the Association of Bridal Consultants. To receive a free printout of consultants in your area, write to 200 Chestnutland Road, New Milford, CT 06776-2521 and include your wedding date, phone number, and a stamped, self-addressed envelope.

COMPLICATED BILLING ARRANGEMENTS. The best way to use a wedding consultant is on a flat-fee basis, and there are two ways to do that:

(a) Shortly after becoming engaged, some couples hire a consultant for a single session that typically lasts about three hours and costs about three hundred dollars. The purpose is simply to decide on the game plan—to get down to the business of creating a schedule, drawing a floor plan, hammering out a budget. It's useful for identifying problems, finding consensus, and coming to grips with such sobering details as the actual eighty-seven-cent cost of mailing each wedding invitation (two twenty-nine-cent stamps because it's so heavy; another for the response card). This consultation gets you started.

(b) Other couples prefer to continue with the wedding planner right up to and through the wedding day. The fee for this package, including the initial session, should run to no more than 15 to 20 percent of the total budget.

PERSONAL INCOMPATIBILITY. The wedding consultant's most important task is roughly equivalent to that of General Eisenhower at Normandy: to land a personal dream on the sandy beaches of reality. Along with organizational skills, this takes patience, cunning, the ability to listen (and quite possibly,

several well-positioned tanks). A good consultant is a buffer between you and the vendors, you and your stepparents, you and
your in-laws, you and your groom, you and your fantasies. Not
that you'd ever—*ever*—use her home phone as a crisis hotline,
but you're going to have to be able to talk to her about everything
from your idea for lighting the ice sculpture with battery packs to
your concern about bathroom accessibility for your grandmother's
wheelchair. She just must be simpatico.

SIXTEEN INSIDE TIPS FROM CERTIFIED WEDDING CONSULTANTS

The voices of experience: Bobbi Ernst, of June Wedding, in San Francisco; Kelly Gladder and Annena Sorenson, of Tie the Knot, in Palo Alto, California; Bea Hoelle, of Bridal Elegance by Bea, in Longwood, Florida; Michelle Lehnen, of Party Palace, in Chattanooga, Tennessee; Christie Rust, of Top of the Plaza, in Chicago:

1   It's more cost-effective to put your money into food and bev-
erages than flowers.
2   Interfaith weddings usually seem happier on neutral ground
—a club, a hotel, a historic site.
3   You'll be sorry if you omit the stamped response card from
the invitation. Many people just don't understand that any invitation carries the obligation to reply.
4   In planning, always start by talking about what you can afford, rather than what you'd like to buy. Vendors may expect to
negotiate.
5   The gown of your dreams should be your first concern, and
your photographer should be the very best you can find. You'll be

looking at those pictures for years, so you want to be captured at your most exquisite.

6 You can save money by having your wedding in a hotel. Hotels already have all the staff and supplies you need, and often they're looking for business on weekends.

7 Set a tone for the wedding that holds all of its elements together. Is it formal or informal? Brunch, evening, or cocktails? Outdoors or inside?

8 Serving only hors d'oeuvres can end up being more expensive than a sit-down meal. With hors d'oeuvres, people never put down their drinks, and it's the liquor that costs. Plus, people pile their little plates with hors d'oeuvres and don't eat half of them.

9 Get plenty of sleep the week before the wedding. That's when major personality changes tend to set in.

10 A big home wedding is work. You have to think about traffic flow, parking, bathrooms, amplified music in a residential area, extra lighting, blowing fuses, the weather, the neighbors, and bugs and bees.

11 The trend is toward formal weddings, but that's a little bit too bad because less formal celebrations would be much more appropriate for so many people.

12 Look for hidden costs. People call them delivery fees, overtime fees, corkage fees, cake-cutting fees. Also, make sure you understand how the gratuities and taxes are computed.

13 Always be sure there's a cancellation clause, and pay a deposit to ensure it. Even *your* wedding could be called off. It happens more than you'd expect, for all sorts of reasons.

14 The delivery date for the gowns should be several weeks before the ceremony.

15 Control the guest list! If people don't respond, phone them to find out if they're coming; if they say they're coming and bringing a date or their children, tell them you're sorry but you're working with limitations that won't permit it.

16 Stick to the budget! Otherwise, you may wind up taking out a loan to pay for your wedding, which is not a good way to start married life.

Traditional Burden Sharing

BRIDE'S FAMILY—OR BRIDE HERSELF —PAYS FOR:

- Her blood test
- Invitation ensemble
- Wedding dress and accessories
- Flowers for maid of honor, bridesmaids, flower girls
- Flowers for church and reception hall
- Engagement and wedding photographs
- Rental fee for marriage site
- Church musicians' fee
- Limo for bridal party to church and reception
- Reception
- Groom's ring if he wears one
- Wedding gift for groom
- Gifts for bride's attendants

GROOM'S FAMILY—OR GROOM HIMSELF—PAYS FOR:

- Bride's engagement and wedding rings
- His blood test and the marriage license
- Fee for person who performs ceremony
- Bride's flowers, corsages for mothers, boutonnieres for groomsmen
- Wedding gift for bride
- Gifts for the best man and the ushers
- Rehearsal dinner
- Honeymoon

81

New, Trendier Burden Sharing

- Groom's parents pay for everything because bride was raised by single working mother who is dirt poor as a result.
- Bride and groom plan everything together, split costs down middle, pay for it all on their own, because he's fifty-seven and she's forty-three and they can take care of themselves.
- Bride pays for everything because groom was in Saudi and blew even his hazardous-duty pay at mall in Riyadh during six-month wait.
- Groom pays for reception because he's a control freak and it's just easier this way, as long as he can have band he wants.

Q: How could we possibly spend from $25,000 to $35,000 to be married? A: Easily. It's the cost of the average urban wedding.

It may cost $15,000, on the average, to have a wedding for 150–200 guests in some rural and suburban areas of the country, but in the Big City the tab is likely to be higher. Consultant Robbi Ernst, of June Wedding, in San Francisco, believes brides should be educated to the realities. Robbi's estimate for the wedding with 150 guests:

ITEM	PRICE
Bridal gown	$700–$3,000
Caterer	$7,500–approximately $12,000 ($50–$75 per person); figure 43 percent of the budget
Photographer	$1,400–$2,000
Flowers	$2,000–$6,000
Band	$1,500–$2,500
Videographer	$1,100–$2,000
Invitations	$600–$800
Rehearsal dinner	$700–$800 (twenty guests, $35–$40 per person)
Clergyperson	$150–$300
Reception site	$1,500–$2,000
Valet parking	$400–$500
Cake	$750–$900
Music at ceremony	$350–$400
Consultant's fee	$300–$4,000

NOTE: *This does not cover the cost of the engagement and wedding rings, the bridesmaids' and mother-of-the-bride's dresses, the prenuptial parties, the attendants' gifts, the honeymoon.*

Q: How can we possibly have a wedding for $7,000–$9,000? A: By sacrificing a few things.

ROBBI SUGGESTS:
• Invite the same number of guests, but on the invitation specify a tea or cocktail reception so no one expects a meal.
• Party for two to three hours instead of five or six. You'll cut the service costs—from the caterer, to the musicians, to the photographer.
• Have the reception at home or at the church or synagogue—or anywhere you don't have to pay an exorbitant site fee.
• Put your money into your dress and the cake, and cut back on liquor.

Q: Can we do anything at all for $5,000? A: Yes, but cut that guest list down to fifty!

THE OFFICIANT'S FEE

The fee to the clergyperson can run approximately $10 to $100. It's traditionally paid by the groom. He should ask about it in advance and give the check to the best man, who presents it the day of the wedding. Couples who are members of the church usually are not charged for its use, but many brides and grooms like to make a donation anyway, often doubling the officiant's fee. Couples who are not members of the church should expect to pay an additional fee for using it—anywhere from just over $100 to just over $1,000.

hese things happen, so don't let them. Instead, plan ahead; deal with established vendors; put everything in writing; understand what happens if you cancel. The list of horrors to avoid:

• The bridal consultant takes your check and leaves town.

• The stationer misspells the groom's name on the invitations.

• The reception hall you reserved is given to another couple who pay extra—and your deposit isn't returned.

• Your wedding gown isn't finished. (Maybe it was never started?)

• Your wedding gown is white, but you ordered ecru.

• The flowers that are delivered don't look anything like the ones in the florist's album.

• The limousine fails to call for the bride and her father.

• The band that shows up isn't as big as you'd expected. And maybe it doesn't know the songs you requested. In fact, maybe the "band" is a disc jockey with tapes.

• The photographer is great, and here—but not for long; he leaves before the cake is cut.

• The pictures don't turn out.

• The cake has three tiers instead of the two you ordered, and you're charged accordingly.

• The tent is filthy.

• The hotel where you planned to honeymoon is overbooked when you arrive.

CROWD PLEASER

 ccording to estimates, an average two hundred guests were invited to each of the 2.5 million weddings held in the United States in 1991. Why is the big wedding so obviously here to stay? Some theories:

THE SEXUAL REVOLUTION. If couples no longer wait to consummate their love, they don't mind being engaged practically forever. And being engaged practically forever gives them plenty of time to plan a really great party.

THE FEMINIST REVOLUTION. Since the bride is a peer, she's working. If she's working she not only has money of her own to contribute to a blowout but also colleagues she has to invite. That it took her until age thirty to achieve such status means there are lots of them.

THE EIGHTIES. Yuppies had money to lavish on such ostentatious displays of consumption as dressing up in fancy clothes and inviting all their friends over to eat and drink the finest foods and wines while dancing to the music of a big band.

THE BREAKDOWN OF THE NUCLEAR FAMILY. Given the size and permutations of certain blended families, two hundred invitations may not be enough to cover it.

MURPHY'S LAW. As applied to a wedding, it means the thing will just get bigger. And bigger. And *bigger*.

A software program called *Celebrate!* by Ergosoft Inc. helps track invitations, gifts, and thank-you notes, and can produce diskettes of guest lists from which stationers can print up invitations and envelopes. It's compatible with certain IBM and IBM-compatible microcomputers. Retail price: $50. For more information, call ErgoSoft at 301-381-5599.

MAKING THE SHORT(?) LIST

Inviting the Guests

 t's easy to get together one hundred or so wedding guests if you (a) come from a traditional nuclear family that gets along; (b) don't have a disproportionately weighty number of cousins; (c) have pathetically few—in fact, perhaps *no*—friends.

Tamper with this formula at all—say, by owning a bulging Rolodex, being wildly popular, or having stepparents—and chances are you will at least once threaten to call off the wedding before you so much as send out the invitations. Most experts suggest starting with the budget and figuring out your guest list from there. (When you see how quickly adding just one guest can run up the cost, you may begin talking about people as "heads" in ways you never have before.) To become selective, simply split the allotment, half to the bride's family and half to the groom's (or the new way: one-third to the bride's parents; one-third to the groom's parents; and one-third to the bridal couple). Next, according to the very general guidelines listed below in descending order of importance, write out the meager few names you can have. Then, start cutting.

1 *The people you absolutely have to invite.* Your parents and siblings and the clergyperson.
2 *People you should invite.* Adult relatives. Create a consistent cutoff point and stick to it—e.g., second cousins. The cutoff point cannot be who's nice versus who isn't. And do not gamble that one branch of the family won't even hear about the wedding (your mother's sister from Albuquerque has to be invited if any of your other aunts is, even if they're all from Boston and she's not.)
3 *People you want to invite.* Your friends. The cutoff point here is emotional, which is to say that drawing up a guest list is a bit like convening a mental encounter group. How *good* a friend is this person? Ask yourself that. Then ask yourself if she sees your relationship the same way. Do your best to be objective.

4 *Your friends' fiancés and live-in companions.* It's a big, cruel world; single people are always being taxed unfairly. Nevertheless, remember the cost per head and ask yourself whether you want to commit to spending $100 to $200 on someone your friend has just met and may have broken up with by the time of the wedding. It's true this is an area where you can make a lot of enemies, but stick to your principles, whatever they are. And if you're *not* including a guest's boyfriend who doesn't live with her, consider calling her up to chat about it before sending the invitation. To soften the blow and all.

5 *Other significant adults.* A former teacher, your parents' next-door neighbors from when you were growing up in the old neighborhood, one of your friends from the senior citizen center where you volunteer—like that.

6 *Children.* Pick an age cutoff—thirteen, or even eighteen. Everyone will be furious, but that's the way it is. Tell them you know they understand.

7 *People from the office.* Considering they are the ones you Xerox with, drink coffee with, stay late with, and debrief about the coup with, a lot of them are already in category 3; conversely, if any of them is already in category 3, study the situation very closely, so as not to cause slights that come back to haunt you. And remember the joke about the merger (manager to secretary: "If my boss calls, get his name")—if you have a boss, invite him.

8 *Friends of friends.* You met them at a party once and sort of liked them. The truth is you probably should *not* invite them—it's too awkward. If they're so great, wait until after you're married and have them over for dinner sometime. And if you're really just thinking about networking at your own wedding, control yourself.

A bride reigns comfortably in the realm of fantasy. The guest treads there awkwardly. Still, she's coming. (You were camp counselors together and you've been corresponding ever since—of course she's coming!) And she has her own hopes for this wedding:

OUT-OF-TOWN GUEST HOPES	WHAT ACTUALLY HAPPENS
Flight will be smooth	Flight is aborted after losing an engine and doing 180 back to airport; guest is forced to miss cocktail party given by your parents' next-door neighbors
To follow your handmade map of your hometown and its interesting tourist attractions	Goes wrong direction on Beltway; spends 1½ hours completing circle, instead of normal 8 minutes for portion of it
To get out of this wedding on the cheap	Spends $1,000 for plane tickets, car rental, hotel room, new outfit, wedding present
To look stunning	Catches rearview glimpse of herself in mirror that reveals she could lose thirty pounds
To meet man of her dreams	Meets your Uncle Herman

THE HIDDEN AGENDA

Dealing with the Invitation

oon into her engagement, a bride may wish to slip into a tony department store or stationer's to check out the samples in those heavy wedding albums she's eyed all her life, imagining her own name in place of Miss Felicity Weatherston's. Alternatively, she may phone several 800 numbers, requesting every single one of the stationery kits advertised in the bridal magazines, thus allowing her home to be leafleted with countless deckled, pearlized, and embossed examples of invitations, cards, napkins, and matches.

Remembering that for an informal wedding of fewer than fifty people it is perfectly correct to write out your own invitations on plain stationery, and recalling at all times that there are so many books on the etiquette of the invitation that it would be pointless to review the rules for wording here, suffice it to say: watch what you say and how you say it on your invitations; it tells a lot. Guests not only learn date, time, and place of the ceremony and reception but also take other cues from the wedding ensemble. (The ensemble is the technical term for everything that falls out of the envelope—from the invitation to the ceremony, to such additional enclosures as the map of Boston with the precisely clocked mileage from the church to the boat in the harbor where the reception will be held—God, our prayers, and the weather willing.) Your choices of paper stock, printing method, typeface, and phrasing speak volumes—and all in fourteen lines, unless you're willing to pay the printer for extra copy, which you may well have to if you intend to add your stepmother as a sponsor. (A sponsor is a person giving the wedding—a host or hostess.)

A formal wedding invitation is engraved or thermographed on heavy white or ecru paper, with a classic script or manuscript. It allows you to reveal yourself as supremely refined and divine (and may somewhat remind power brides of their engraved business cards, the little ones that have their names and the words Senior Vice President for Development). The formal wedding invitation follows such strict convention that at first it may seem difficult to compose correctly, but in fact—just as when a bride writes a good memo or novel—the thing is freeing: it liberates you from blunders and allows you to extend a completely impeccable greeting to almost anyone you can think of. A formal invitation is not only a relief for you, but comfort for your guests. Receiving it is for them something like sighting the waving semaphores of a rescue ship. That's because they need only to read between your very precise fourteen lines to understand precisely what to expect: a formal wedding, start to finish. What to wear, what to give you, how to entertain you has already been signaled; therefore, everyone can relax and have a good time. (*Note:* If you are sending formal invitations, be sure you have everything the way you want

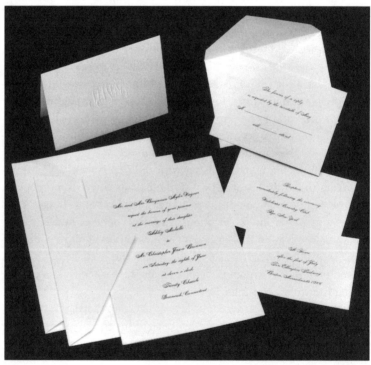

PHOTO COURTESY CRANE AND CO.

it before you give the okay to the printer—errors in etiquette are redone on your nickel.)

In recent years, however, partly as a result of the changing nature of the family and society, and partly because of the burgeoning number of weddings, there has been a proliferation of alternative, even lighthearted, informal wedding stationery. Brides are embracing recyclable materials, zippy inks, inspired messages—in a subliminal display of the more relaxed, jokey, and fun-loving sides of their personalities. The technically proficient bride uses her computer for a dazzling trompe l'oeil wonder of an invitation; the New Age bride, psychedelic colors on a resilient tissue paper; the craftsy bride, potato printing. The idea is to keep things simple and whimsical, and to ask your little brother to do his best writing on the envelopes so he won't feel left out. Guests receiving an informal invitation understand they're in for an unconventional time and prepare accordingly, even if it means buying a pair of hiking boots to wear to your wedding in the woods. (*Note:* Even if you're making your own invitations, assemble about twenty-five more than you'll need for your guest list, just as you would if you were having them printed—there are always mistakes.)

Addressing hundreds of envelopes for invitations and announcements is a task that can span a full two weeks. Brides hire a calligrapher or rent videotapes of movies about weddings—*Father of the Bride*; *A Wedding*; *True Love*; *Betsy's Wedding*—to watch while they work. If you're doing things the usual way, you'll order invitations three months before the ceremony, and mail them six to eight weeks prior to it. Once they're issued, it's natural to await the replies with some eagerness. They give shape to the wedding, supplying you with such vital information as head count and the identity of those who will actually be sharing your day with you.

Rule of Thumb: No matter how much you spend on the invitations and stationery, it's not as much as you'll spend on the flowers.

REGISTER HERE

The Wedding Presents

OVERVIEW. Originally, wedding presents signaled a truce between the conquering hero and the bride's father, but as marriage by capture evolved into marriage by purchase, the gifts became more obviously associated with the price the groom was paying for the bride. Later, everyone got into the act, with the result that if you are a wedding guest today you may send something (salt and pepper shakers are always useful) to the bride and groom as soon as you receive the invitation—and you must do so within one year of the date of the wedding. There is a practice in some cultures of keeping a written record of each gift's value, so that when a gift must be given in return it is precisely equivalent. (And there is a practice at some gift registries of messing things up so the bride receives not one but six espresso makers. Proceed with caution.)

HOW TO USE A BRIDAL REGISTRY. Register at least three months before the wedding.

Don't register at a store you would never patronize in your nonbridal life. If you do, the chances are good that not only will you be uncomfortable—and you're going to have to be there for several hours, probably on at least two occasions—but also that your guests will be. Call the stores you're considering and ask for the complimentary packet for brides; it usually includes a catalogue with pictures of the registry's gifts, and will help you decide whether to go any further.

Use your first trip to the store to confront the decisions to be made regarding sheets and towels and can openers and electronic equipment and whatever else the registry roster lists among its literally hundreds of items. Wait until your second trip to tell the registry consultant (who was undoubtedly too busy to sit with you the first time, while you fantasized) what you would like.

Most registries have a table handy so you can play with your table setting. Do it. Don't try to assemble it all in your head.

Don't register for things you don't really want—you run the risk of receiving them instead of what you prefer.

PHOTO BY JOSH HASKIN COURTESY OF TIFFANY & CO.

Don't try to select everything in one day if you're starting to see double.

Do register for some inexpensive items unless you want your guests to spend more than they'd like, even on you.

Do take your groom with you at least once (unless, as comedian Cindy Eaton puts it, he'll fear things are getting too serious if you're picking a china pattern). Also take your mother, your sister, your friends, or anyone else who wants to come on a jaunt to the bridal registry. In fact, take whomever you want, whenever you like. There is no wrong way to choose water goblets.

Do inquire about the computer system. Will your selections be on line at the Chicago store as well as the Philadelphia branch?

Don't be cowed. You may have been raised to believe every bride has a china, silver, and crystal pattern—and yet secretly suspect that with years of field work ahead of you as an expert on the Australian outback you may not be giving formal dinner parties for twelve all that often. Think it through.

HOW NOT TO USE A BRIDAL REGISTRY. Some brides claim a conscientious-objector status regarding gift registries. They feel they'd rather be surprised and touched by the footstool Great-aunt Lillian comes up with, having removed it from storage upon realizing that at last someone in this family other than herself appreciates fine antiques. Or by the silver platter from the guys in the groom's fantasy baseball league. Or by anything anyone wants to give, really. Your family and friends

The earliest wedding gifts were tokens the groom bestowed on the bride's furious father. Today's wedding gifts, bestowed on the couple by the wedding guests, are often . . .

CANDLESTICKS
A Ranking

1 Frank Lloyd Wright
2 Chunky crystal
3 Brass
4 Scandinavian design breakthrough requiring eighteen hard-to-find pencil-thin candles
5 Porcelain holders for votive candles (or are they a new kind of egg cup?)
6 Hurricane lamp used in Colonial times, but never in most parts of Denver
7 Heartbreakingly thin glassware that will snap in two during insertion of first candle
8 Witty wire sculpture
9 Saucer/receptacle thing for stout sixties-type multicolor scented candle
10 Ornate silver candelabra with monogram

happen to be capable of thinking for themselves. And it's all so generous.

HOW TO USE THE 800 NUMBERS. Mail-order shopping for wedding gifts is made possible by brides who register with certain stores. For example, Ross-Simons, a three-store chain in Rhode Island, can be accessed nationwide by phoning (800) 556-7376. Using Ross-Simons as the clearinghouse, a bride anywhere in the country can register by phone; gift-givers anywhere in the country can order the same way, using any major credit card. Thus, to select a present for a bride from Cheyenne, a wedding guest from Tampa simply calls the 800 number to ask what she has yet to receive. And if the Cheyenne bride has neglected to register? The Tampa person, knowing her china, crystal, and silver patterns, can order them anyway—Ross-Simons carries the tableware of most famous manufacturers, at a discount, and will fulfill.

DISPLAYING THE BOOTY. How's the security at your mother's place? That's where the gifts should be set out if you wish to observe the ancient custom of putting out the loot for everyone to inspect. Cover a table with a lovely white cloth and display one complete place setting. Mass the other gifts in groupings of related items or all mixed together. Why are you doing this? So everyone can exclaim over your Royal Doulton Cathay, and your demitasse cups, and your crystal jam pot, and the way you mixed two patterned with one plain as no one else ever has before, and so Uncle Herman can figure out how the peanut-butter extruder works.

HOW TO RECEIVE WEDDING PRESENTS AT THE WEDDING RECEPTION.
If you set up a table, they will come. Indeed, if a favorite activity for the out-of-town guest is to hit the mall immediately upon arrival and collect a gift, and if some people just hate the hassle and expense of the post office, or are only now getting around to thinking about this, it follows that quite a few ice buckets and cheese slicers will appear at the wedding itself. Don't open them there. In fact, don't even think about them. According to all the manuals, it's technically the job of a specially designated usher to deal with these offerings. Let him take them back to your mother's house. You go to Oahu.

Six wedding presents for the couple who have been living together for years and/or got the china and silver from a previous marriage.

1 Birdfeeder
2 Copy of *Heloise's Household Hints*
3 Two tickets to a play, ball game, Philadelphia
4 Share of stock that can only go up during course of marriage
5 Massage series (if they like to be touched)
6 Gift certificate to incredibly well-stocked urban deli, such as Zabar's in New York

DUTCH TREAT

The Bridal Shower

PROBLEM: It's sixteenth- or seventeenth-century Holland and you're a young maiden with a boyfriend but no dowry. Your father is a poor miller. He'll never be able to come up with the goods that will make you a viable commodity.

SOLUTION: Elope to a distant land, always remembering that you're a valuable person in your own right and don't need to be effectively sold by your father to your husband just in order to wed. *Or:* Be lucky enough to have friends who take pity on your plight and shower you with enough gifts to constitute a dowry of sorts. Now you can marry. Sisterhood is powerful. Everyone is happy.

The tradition of showers began when a mere handful of little Dutch girls banded together and discovered that in union there is strength. Whether you believe you're committing a political act the next time you attend a bridal shower is up to you, but do ponder—perhaps while the Edible Undies ("sensuous with taste") are being opened—how fulfilling it is to give to others what they want and need. Increasingly, the shower is for the couple, not just the bride, and friends of each gender attend. Shower themes change with the times. Some current favorites:

COVERED DISH. The guests arrive with covered dishes for dinner. After the meal, they are washed—and all of a sudden, the bowls and plates and wine glasses they've brought become the presents.

QUILT. Each guest brings a square worked in a motif relating to the bride and groom. After the squares have been pieced together, the guests convene a second time for an old-fashioned quilting bee.

WISHING WELL. Guests check in with the local bridal registries, to discover the items the couple is wishing for. Would you have guessed an espresso maker? You would? How about the silver-plated garlic press?

BARBECUE. Everyone into the backyard for hamburgers, hot dogs, chicken, beer. The presents are barbecue accessories

Does the bachelorette party threaten the very warp and woof (as it were) of the traditional bachelor party? A comparison of the most popular activities at current.

LAST FLINGS

BACHELOR PARTY	BACHELORETTE PARTY
1 Eating steak	1 Renting pornographic videotape
2 Playing poker	2 Going to male strip show
3 Golfing	3 Going to singles bar
4 Skydiving	4 Showing slides of old boyfriends
5 Drag racing	5 Calling up old boyfriends
6 Attending boxing match	6 Phoning Love Line and meeting
7 Going to dog track	interesting, exciting people
8 Skeet shooting	7 Forcing bride to chugalug
9 Singing	drinks with vulgar names made
10 Giving and receiving	from Kahlúa and Bailey's Irish
usher's gifts	Cream

—those really long forks, baskets filled with condiments, an apron with a slogan.

LINGERIE. For the bride whose life is pictured in the Victoria's Secret catalogue. The bride's bust size is thoughtfully noted on the invitation (and usually ends up being faxed around town). Everyone brings teddies and bras and slips and half-slips and nighties and bustiers and pajamas and garters and panties. There are so many items in this category that it would be exhausting to mention them all.

HANDYCOUPLE. You mainly bring power tools. Ideal for people who watch "This Old House" or have already been living together so long it's time to put on an addition.

OFFICE. Everyone in the department pitches in and buys a Mr. Coffee, or something equally splendid. In some offices the shower givers take the bride out to lunch in a restaurant, where they give her the present; in other offices, the staff breaks at four-thirty for champagne, cake, and the presentation. Invariably, the gift card is designed by the folks in Creative—and signed, high school yearbook fashion, by all.

SPORTSCOUPLE. They're jocks. They met on the tennis court; her idea of fashion is a sweatsuit; his favorite activity usually takes place at the sports arena. Buy them some new exercise outfits, badminton and volleyball sets, beach towels, sports watches, season tickets to the baskets. And now that each of them has a doubles partner for life, get them some new tennis balls, too.

AROUND-THE-CLOCK. Perhaps the most popular at the moment. As many as two dozen friends cover every hour of the day and night with appropriate gifts. Early morning is easy—a toaster. Midnight is fun—there's all that lacy lingerie to choose from. But everyone dreads two o'clock in the afternoon. Think about it: it's possibly the least defined hour in anyone's personal schedule.

Shrink Think 2

What are you going through, now that you're choosing your dress and your attendants? Psychotherapist Karen Faircloth has an empathetic reading of the bride's emotional state.

Dear Therapist Karen:

I'm deeply in love, and have dreamed my whole life of being a bride. But lately I wonder what I'm getting myself into. How do I know whether I can be a good *wife?* I'm so tense that I broke out in hives while my fiancé and I were shopping for a bed yesterday, and this morning we had a fight. Should I cancel the wedding? My fiancé and I could just live together. That's not really what I want, but it might be easier. Plus I absolutely *have* to lose five pounds by next week to fit into my dress. Help! What's happening to me?

Nervous Wreck

Dear Nervous Wreck:

Living together is for kids; marriage is for almost-grownups who want to develop further into responsible adults. Of course you really want to be married, and you are having anxiety about it. This is translated into your doubting yourself. Not only are you wondering if you can be a good wife, but also you're thinking you're imperfect by those five pounds. Self-examination is good; a little stage fright brings out a good performance. Try to tell yourself you're not as good a wife now as you're going to be after practicing in the role. Trust yourself.

Love,
Karen

Chapter Four

ROYAL RAIMENT

BASIC

BRIDAL

CLOTHING

specially dressed bride is the focal point of every wedding. She's the prize, the community's hope for the future. And what she wears and carries—her gown, her veil, her garter, her bouquet—all have meaning. In the beginning, of course, she might have put on just a simple shift for her kidnapping. But as the eons unfolded, her raiment became vastly more glamorous. This is only fair. If the bride is trying to mimic royalty, and the royals are trying to mimic the gods and goddesses (see Praying for Rain: The Myth Behind the Ceremony, page 162), she certainly should have a nice dress for her coronation. Indeed, it is perfectly proper, as the bride comes down the aisle, to turn and gape at just how exquisitely garbed—and how lovely—she is. A wedding allows the spectators to depart reality; the presentation of the bride in her beautiful costume is their trip. She's wearing this extravaganza for everyone.

The veil is another matter. She's wearing that for her husband. Although many experts have believed the bride's veil was meant to protect her against evil spirits, there also seems to be evidence that it derives from the material used to wrap the captive bride-to-be, and eventually told the world she had been sold and that henceforth no man might look upon her but her husband. The veil came to be a disguise the bride could hide behind, and in many parts of the world ultimately gave rise to the practice of the False Bride. According to this custom, an ugly old woman, her face covered in veils, took the place of the true bride during much of the procession through the village to meet the groom. Today's bride may observe a vestige of this tradition by asking her maid of honor to act as her stand-in for at least part of the wedding rehearsal. Not that today's maid of honor is old and ugly, of course —far from it, if only because at a wedding everyone is young and gorgeous.

Especially the bride. That she is young and gorgeous there is just no hiding in the end. Everyone knows it—thus, the garter. It's blue because blue is the color of the Virgin Mary, but long before New Testament times it was a sash worn just below the

Dresses Through the Decades

1900s	1920s	1930s
The Victorian bride covered up with a high-neck, blouson-bodice, floor-length dress.	The Jazz Age bride revealed her ankles for the first time.	The Art Deco bride wore slinky, bias-cut satin.

1940s	1950s
The war bride appeared in a practical suit.	The postwar bride was a princess in a fairytale.

PHOTOS COURTESY SUSAN LANE AND COUNTRY ELEGANCE

Trains, Veils, and Headpieces

A significant encumbrance is not only the best disguise but also beautiful. Anyway, everyone knows you're under there, swathed in the whole nine yards of satin, wrapped in a cocoon of tulle, balancing a simple crown. A fully accessorized wedding dress may be uncomfortable and impractical, but most agree it's the massive touches that make it the most breathtaking outfit in the world. Consider:

Cathedral train for ultraformal wedding.

Chapel train for ultraformal or formal wedding.

PHOTO COURTESY BRIDAL ORIGINALS

PHOTO COURTESY BRIDAL ORIGINALS

Short veil to wear with short dress at semiformal wedding.

PHOTO COURTESY SUSAN LANE AND COUNTRY ELEGANCE

Sweep train for formal evening or daytime wedding.

Long, full-length veil and headpiece for ultraformal wedding.

PHOTO COURTESY JIM HJELM/A PRIVATE COLLECTION

MODEL: PATRICIA GROOME, I.M.G. MODELS, NEW YORK. PHOTO: MEMO ZACK, NEW YORK, FOR PAULA VARSALONA

Shoulder- or fingertip-length veil for formal daytime wedding.

Veil flowing to hem for formal evening wedding.

PHOTO COURTESY DEMETRIOS FOR ILISSA

MODEL: PATRICIA GROOME, I.M.G. MODELS, NEW YORK. PHOTO: MEMO ZACK, NEW YORK, FOR PAULA VARSALONA

bride's knee to keep away the wandering hands of the groom and his men. Somehow it always came undone anyway; some scholars theorize that its loosening symbolized the community's sympathetic efforts to ease the bride's pangs in childbirth. Whatever the case, the removal of the garter often led to a melee reminiscent of marriage by capture. Still, over the centuries the custom survived. Somewhat toned down but still raucous, it's a high point of many contemporary wedding feasts. Usually, the groom does his garter-removing deed against background music with a pulsing beat.

If the bride could use one last thing to hold on to, it probably shouldn't be her bouquet. That's because originally it wasn't made of flowers at all, but of garlic, chives, rosemary, bay leaves, and other strong herbs thought effective in driving away evil spirits. The bride took the bouquet with her to her new home, where she proceeded to set it afire, the better to fumigate the place against bad influences. Then she tossed it to the winds.

Most wedding planners advise taking two hours to dress for your wedding. Considering that you have to fit the heavy weight of history to your shoulders, this only makes sense; take safety pins and masking tape to the bridal room and make alterations where needed.

IF THE SHOE FITS

Just because you're being carried off by a dashing prince doesn't mean you're Cinderella. Still, you'll be more comfortable in your new royal role (not to mention in the receiving line and on the dance floor) . . .

TIMOTHY LEE

he range of bridal footwear is fairly wide and increasingly imaginative, so shop until you find exactly what's right for you. The selection pictured here is from Peter Fox: a classic white brocade pump, which you can have plain or jeweled; a classic white brocade mid-calf boot; and a white satin pump with ribbon ties like a ballet slipper. Each choice starts at somewhat over two hundred dollars, which may seem like a lot to spend on costume shoes, but then again, your flowers are expensive, too, and you can't dye them black later.

General shoe pointers:

• Heels are most comfortable at around two and one-quarter inches.
• To avoid flesh-colored legs, wear off-white, not white, sheer pantyhose with your white dress and white shoes. (And be *sure* to take an extra pair of pantyhose to the dressing room.)
• Skip the galoshes-and-wedding-dress look without ruining your fancy shoes: if the weather is bad, put on an old pair of shoes for the dash to shelter. Switch once you're indoors.

he beautiful bride puts heart, soul, and maybe some whimsy into the finishing touches she scatters about her person. Don't let the incidentals be accidental —plan ahead. From Vera Wang Bridal House, Ltd., some examples of lovely ways to express your individuality on your wedding day. Clockwise:

AN ANTIQUE LINEN AND LACE HANDKERCHIEF. To catch the tears of joy (see page 62) signifying either that you'll never cry in this marriage again or else that the crops will grow. (*Note:* As between these two superstitions, many experienced brides suggest going with the crop belief.)

AN OLD-FASHIONED GARTER. Brocade ribbon and a rosette on the outside. And on the inside? Look for the blue lining.

SIMPLE WHITE KIDSKIN GLOVES. Rather than fussy ones.

ITEMS COURTESY VERA WANG BRIDAL HOUSE, NEW YORK. PHOTO: TIMOTHY LEE

PEARL BRACELET.
The traditional bridal love of pearls can be indulged these days as never before, because strides in the manufacture of costume jewelry have made it difficult to tell the difference between something quite affordable and something severely out of the question. Brides are mixing their millimeters (means the size of the pearl), perhaps wearing large pearls at the throat, medium ones on their ears, smaller ones at the wrist. The trick to pulling together a total look? Coordinate the clasps—rhinestones with rhinestones; gold with gold, etc.

PEARL EARRINGS.
These pretty drop pearls swing gently, look pretty with almost any current hair style, and aren't at all heavy (thank you, costume pearl processors).

SINGLE STRAND OF PEARLS.
Decorative but not overwhelming.

IT ISN'T EASY WEARING GREEN

The Color of Your Gown

 he bride wears white because brides have always worn white, and always will. Correct?

Not exactly. Historically, brides have worn whatever color suited them best—in fact, the only truly unacceptable color for a bridal dress is green, which is pretty much taboo everywhere except Norway. (Why blackball green? There are several explanations. Some insist green is reserved for fairies; some say it's the color of jealousy; some argue that green hints at grass stains, and grass stains hint at an illicit premarital sex romp.) Precedent is plentiful for wearing a color other than white on your wedding day. Consider: Chinese brides wear red, the color of happiness. Spanish peasant brides and Icelandic brides wear black. In ancient Rome, yellow was the wedding color. During the American Revolution, brides occasionally appeared in red, to signify rebellion; otherwise in the eighteenth century, brides dressed mostly in yellow and blue. In Civil War times, a bride might put on purple, to signify mourning for her father killed in action.

The white dress is basically a Victorian development. What's more, during the reign of that most powerful, monarch, wearing bridal white had connotations of affluence; it's only since the turn of the century that the idea of white as a sign of purity has taken precedence. Use this fact. Wear white only because you choose to. Don't wear it if you don't want to. (It tends to drain color from an older face.) Do wear it if others don't want you to, and you do. (Pre–Queen Victoria, white had the connotation of joy—and you're joyful, aren't you?) A nineteenth-century verse laying out an array of options and their consequences survives today:

> *Married in white, you have chosen right,*
> *Married in green, ashamed to be seen,*
> *Married in gray, you will go far away,*
> *Married in red, you will wish yourself dead,*
> *Married in blue, love ever true,*
> *Married in yellow, you're ashamed of your fellow,*
> *Married in black, you will wish yourself back,*
> *Married in pink, of you he'll aye think.*

DRESSED TO WED

The Ten Organizing Themes of the Bride's and Groom's Apparel

 t's easy to pick the bridal couple out of a crowd. That's because they stand head and shoulders above it. They're monarchs, imperial and divine. That brides tend to a certain sameness (and grooms to occasional follies) in their look can't be helped. Dominion notwithstanding, the bride and groom are slaves to a dress code decreed by centuries of status. If you are what you wear, in your clothes you are:

1 A DREAM WALKING. The bridal gown may be flashy, refined, beaded, tasteful, ridiculous, heart-stopping, adorable, white, or nonwhite, but it always has the aura of splendor. As a result, the bride may wear her grandmother's remodeled shift, originally made from an old curtain during the depths of the Great Depression, and be convinced she is glorious; everyone present will agree. As well, in recent years the groom has come to insist on staging a little fashion show of his own. Whereas once upon a time he contented himself with a shy-guy look, dressing in a morning coat, a uniform, a dark business suit, he's now more apt to stick a colorful handkerchief into his pocket.

2 A PERFECT FIT. Whether the bride's costume has a nipped-in waist and full skirt or follows the silhouette from *Splash* does not matter; it fits. She stood on a box while someone with pins in her mouth made sure of that. Similarly, her groom has gone through the whole inseam routine.

3 SPOTLESS. A bride may ordinarily never be far from a cup of coffee, but dressed to wed she wouldn't touch the stuff— at least until the reception. As she is victorious and unbowed in love, so is her dress unsullied.

4 UNWRINKLED. The person who does not sit does not get creases. Therefore, the bride either chooses a bustle or train she can move to one side or, riding over to the ceremony in a limo, approaches the backseat as though she were a Hovercraft. Many brides in finery prefer the ancient tradition of walking through the streets to the ceremony; some brides are literally steamed just

before they walk down the aisle. Grooms merely trust the rental place to put creases where they belong and not where they don't.

5 MAJESTIC. When it requires several small boys and girls to keep your train on track as you move down the aisle, a certain slowness infects the mood; things turn weighty, solemn, awe-inspiring. Likewise, when the chosen accessory of the groom is a jeweled saber (see The Military Wedding, page 146).

6 SELFISH. With only a few exceptions, the bride will never wear her dress again, and neither will anyone else. It will hang in her closet for her children to admire, or—in the rare instance—in the Smithsonian for the nation to admire. And while the groom's clothing may be eminently recyclable (if it was rented), no one will ever wear it again with the same generous charm.

7 SERIOUSLY EMBELLISHED. The bride, with beads, sequins, seed pearls. The groom, with a not-too-little boutonniere in the wedding colors of peach and purple.

8 AN EXAMPLE TO ALL. Note how the attendants strive to look young and gorgeous too. Even though they don't have as much to work with.

9 NOT REALLY ALL THAT SEXY. Unless you choose Bob Mackie as your outfitter.

10 FASCINATING. Designed with a keyhole to reveal her shoulder blades, the bride's gown even has back interest. And the groom's black shoes are so shiny you can almost see your reflection in them. These are clothes for display, totally extravagant, thoroughly entertaining. As metal filings to a magnet, all eyes are drawn to them. They are the center of attention.

n some ways it may seem wiser to borrow your mother's wedding dress, rent a stranger's, or sew your own—but most brides buy theirs. They take on this challenge as an almost holy quest. And why not?

If the bridal dress is the sine qua non that encapsulates and expresses not only your private fantasies but the community's . . .

If it is the baptismal garment that clothes you during your transition from a previous existence to a new life . . .

If it's something everyone is going to see you in, something that's going to be around in pictures, and on video, for the rest of your days, it should be just right, exactly what you want. It should be *you*.

Or at least you as a top model in the pages of *Bride's* or *Modern Bride*. That's where you may first spy the dress that catches your fancy. Let's say it's about eight months before your wedding, which is when most brides begin shopping for their dresses. What do you do? You rip the page from the magazine and try, perhaps, to phone the manufacturer (who will not sell to you directly no matter what you do, not even if you present yourself in person at 1385 Broadway; and who will shriek at you "We don't deal with the public!" if you call on the phone; and who might nevertheless be able to cut a deal with your uncle in the business, but that's a special case we're not at liberty to discuss). Now you look at the ad again, and there you see the Available at These and Other Fine Stores list, and so you head out to the nearest venue. Marketing studies show that while you may not end up deciding on the dress you sought, you will probably find a dress you want. And having found it, you won't go elsewhere. You'll buy it. That's why stores insist on protection from, and advertising by, the manufacturers. There are three main types of stores:

THE BRIDAL SALON. Sixty-two percent of all brides buy their gowns at bridal shops, according to a survey by *Modern Bride* magazine; brides try on an average of eight

1 "Sometimes I think it's the mother who's getting married."
2 "The friction—I hate it. I hate the mothers."
3 "I'm resigned to them. It's just that they're awful."

dresses at four salons. Not all bridal shops are alike—between Renee Strauss in Beverly Hills and Miss Manfuga's Bridal Shop in Manhattan, there's not just a country but a world of difference —but as most are specialty shops selling only bridal merchandise, they can be assumed to have at least a bit of special expertise. What's more, some are able not only to remove stress, a feature that's especially appealing to working women, but also to provide comfort. Vera Wang Bridal House, in New York, even offers low-fare hotel packages for clients coming for appointments from out of town.

You may pay more at a bridal shop; when you do, it's said to be for the selection of merchandise as well as for the hands-on attention, excellent alterations, and somewhat firmer guarantee your dress will actually be delivered to you on time. Look, why should you be expected to have an eye for fashion? (This is how the argument goes.) Do you have an ear for music? (If you do, the analogy breaks down somewhat, but anyway, you get the drift of the rhetoric.) Only certain people are gifted. Therefore, you're wise to entrust yourself to an establishment whose buyers know how to purchase judiciously and edit accordingly. They will present only the choicest creations to you, and as an extra bonus may even help you pull together the total, accessorized look

A sales representative who travels the country offering the bridal gowns of a famous manufacturer characterizes today's brides:

THE REGIONAL BRIDE

NEW YORK
HAS THE OLDEST BRIDES.

ST. LOUIS
HAS THE SHORTEST BRIDES.

CHICAGO
HAS THE PRETTIEST BRIDES.

ATLANTA
HAS THE YOUNGEST BRIDES.

HOUSTON
HAS THE BRIDES WITH THE
BIGGEST BOSOMS.

you've carried in your head practically since infancy but haven't quite been able to articulate until now. In short, on your wedding day you'll be so smashing, so special, that you'll leave every other bride since the beginning of time in the dust.

Note: Certain high-end shops tend to make a big fuss about the exclusive, or "one of a kind" dress. Apparently, it is designed for the woman who fears she's in danger of meeting herself coming down the street in her wedding gown. Or who can't bear the idea of finding her maid of honor dressed in the same style at *her* wedding. Or who will not recover upon discovering another photo on the society page almost identical to hers. For exclusivity, you pay extra. A lot extra.

THE DEPARTMENT STORE. Perhaps as part of an overall consumer trend, brides are not buying their dresses here as frequently as they might; they're shopping in specialty stores instead. The rap against the bridal department: it missed the boat. Critics say this is mostly a matter of merchandising. That is, when the department store's natural customer turns to its bridal department, she typically finds it tucked away, cramped, and hard to use. Items she might want to buy with her gown—shoes, undergarments, a handkerchief, for example—are scattered all over the store. Worse, especially for the working woman, service takes forever and is not particularly (or at all) knowledgeable. And bridesmaids' dresses are not usually available.

However! Department stores

A NATION OF BRIDAL
SHOPKEEPERS

*Fine Stores Across
the Country:*

ATLANTA
Anne Barge for Brides
(404-237-0898)

BALTIMORE
Leo Amster Ltd.
(301-296-8383)

CHICAGO
Eva's Bridals and Fashions
(312-777-3111)

DALLAS
Mockingbird Bridal Boutique
(214-823-6873)

DENVER
A Wedding Showcase
(303-935-2444)

KANSAS CITY
Schaffer's Bridal Shop
(816-756-4600)

LOS ANGELES
Renee Strauss for the Bride
(213-653-3331)
Wilshire Bridal Salon
(213-388-2297)

NEW YORK
Kleinfeld's
(718-833-1100)
Vera Wang Bridal House
(212-490-1100)

SAN FRANCISCO
Bridal Galleria
(415-346-6160)

often accept co-op advertising dollars from manufacturers. As a result, a store in your area may well advertise bridal previews. These are the "trunk" shows so worth attending. Go. Worst case, you'll see samples of beautiful dresses at price points you can't afford, and make alternate plans. Best case, you'll get some advice from the manufacturer's rep, come across a wonderful gown you can charge, fall in with a sympathetic and experienced salesperson—and come up a winner. Department stores also have sales, usually in August. In Boston, check out Filene's the day after Thanksgiving, too. And in Birmingham, Michigan, keep your eye on Jacobsen's year round—the bridal department is well stocked and the sales tax is a mere 4 percent.

THE DISCOUNT HOUSE. A discount house *hates* to be called that. And don't refer to it as low end, either. More politely, say it's efficient. Which it is. A discount house is all about time and space: the more square footage it has, the faster its stock must be turned. This is not the place to have a cozy chat about the feminine myth and its perpetuation with you in the starring role. This is the place that sells from stock, right off the rack. Within a span of hours, it is possible to try on a wedding gown here, take it with you, and wear it to be married. Obviously, there won't be a whole lot of alterations or service in such a transaction, but if you're a perfect size, know what you want, and are in a hurry, this could be for you.

A TRIP TO KLEINFELD'S

Kleinfeld's is the famous bridal boutique in Brooklyn, New York. You can be there in only an hour if you take the R train from Manhattan or a cab in from the airport. Brides come from around the globe to buy their gowns at Kleinfeld's—some eight thousand a year for twenty-five years, to be exact. It's arguably the world's largest bridal shop. A friend writes:

It was eleven o'clock on a Tuesday morning in autumn and, to use an inelegant phrase, the joint was jumping. As far as the eye could see, each of the twenty-five fitting rooms at Kleinfeld's was occupied not only by a bride, but also by her mother, maybe a friend, and a sales consultant. (When you make your appointment, you're assigned a representative who personally oversees your order from the moment you first try to explain what you have in mind right through to your selection, accessorizing, and final fitting.) Kleinfeld's carries 800–1,000 dresses in stock at any one time, with new styles arriving every day. "Our gowns range from the mid-priced to the finest," co-owner Hedda Schacter told me. "We stress quality. We work with the designers."

Indeed. There was a Diamond Collection trunk show the morning I was there. Designer Robert Legere watched as brides tried on his creations and swept out of their fitting rooms to study themselves in the mirrored wall of the central hallway. "Is it too plain?" one bride asked. She was wearing a raw silk gown with a pleated portrait collar and sleeves. "I'm not a beaded person," she said, "but is this too—?"

Legere broke in, to talk about why he likes to emphasize structure and shape, rather than "beads and busyness that take away from you."

The bride was loving that dress.

"You make a simple dress your own by wearing sparkling earrings, a formal hairstyle," Legere suggested.

"Yes," agreed the bride. "Yes."

If she ended up buying that gown, she paid about $1,300 (price tags are coded; look for the middle digits) instead of approximately $1,400 elsewhere. There are definite savings at Kleinfeld's. "We have a very fair pricing schedule," said Hedda Schacter, "but I don't like to speak of discounts." Whatever. I saw a Scaasi dress with a heavily jeweled long-sleeved top and tulle skirt—"Glamour," it's called—for $2,995. Two weeks earlier, I'd seen it in Washington, D.C., at Woodward & Lothrop, for $3,800.

All morning, Miss Hedda (as her staff calls her) was on the go, issuing instructions, scoldings, greetings, compliments. The air in the shop is charged, the noise level high. Nothing gets in the way of the business at hand. Gorgeous models in high-fashion makeup swirl their skirts and trains past stacks of cardboard cartons. Sales representatives, fitters, and headpiece experts scurry for stock. A father stands beaming in the hallway, trying to stay out of the way. If you can't find the dress you want here, and quickly, it's hard to imagine where you will. This is no-nonsense, no-frills, lots of merchandise. The best pun to make about Kleinfeld's? Don't turn down the volume. The shop carries every name-brand designer you've ever heard of (and then some—imports included), frequently offering new styles before they are seen elsewhere at retail. This is the place for silk, for antique lace—for the latest and most up-to-date in the oldest and most traditional.

Kleinfeld's, 8202 Fifth Avenue, Brooklyn, NY 11209 (718) 833-1100. Open until 6:00 P.M. Wednesday, Friday, Saturday, and 9:00 P.M. Tuesday and Thursday; closed Sunday and Monday. Phone for directions.

WHO IS DEMETRIOS?

PHOTO COURTESY DEMETRIOS FOR ILISSA

rides read *Bride's*—four million of them every issue. Do four million women a month wonder about Demetrios? Probably. It would be difficult not to—he takes fifty pages of ads in every magazine. Demetrios for Ilissa . . . brides know the signature phrase. (They also know his signature—it has that lingering *s* that trails after his name like a banner in the breeze.)

Demetrios is fortyish, married, with two children. He has a pleasant face, a mustache, and a pony tail. He left Piraeus, in Greece, when he was seventeen and settled in Warren, Ohio, where his mother opened a bridal shop. There he learned the basics of the retailing business—and experimented with a youthful brainstorm: advertising her shop in *Bride's*.

His mother's business skyrocketed. (These days she has a new boutique, Matina's Bridal Collection, in Winter Haven, Florida; it sells only Ilissa.)

Demetrios went to New York. He bought the name Ilissa from a relatively obscure dress manufacturer and set to work. From the beginning, he advertised. He did something else, too:

His Video

Offstage breezes blow gusts of wind at a model apparently doing neck-relaxation exercises. She doesn't speak. She inhales deeply. She looks as if she might have a fever. In the background is the sound of wind and string instruments, as in a dentist's office. Sometimes there is near-dead silence—have we lost the patient?—until the music resumes. The viewer, accustomed to a faster pace on TV, may find herself waiting for things to pick up. Then she gets it: *she has died and gone to heaven.* For forty-

He married the bride's dream and the American Dream.

That's why the fifty pages; that's why the beads; that's why the affordable ($500 and up) price points; that's why if you can fantasize it he will make it. Demetrios gowns are democratic. In America, every woman has the right to be a princess. It's in the Constitution.

Or at least if Demetrios had his way it would be. Life, liberty, the pursuit of happiness, and a royal wedding—that's how it would go. Demetrios believes women hold their bridal fantasies very close, that when they walk into a bridal shop they already know what they want. They've known for years; it has nothing to do with the winds of fashion. His job is to give it to them. He sees his work as something of a mission—brides need to be brides the way mankind needs to be free. He has silhouettes and body lines to suit everyone: "High necks, low necks, V-necks, long torsos, full skirts—we go after every look." Says Demetrios, there is one time in her life when a woman has a real opportunity to "dress up and show off"—at her wedding. "She shouldn't be in a plain dress."

five minutes, bridal gowns—some sixty or one hundred of them, depending on which tape you have—parade across the screen. Someone sings the "Ave Maria" during the segment on enormous sleeves. Close-ups focus on hips, waistlines, beadwork, trains. There's more. And more. And more. It could go on through all eternity. Dresses are numbered for identification purposes. Call the 800 number and they'll tell you where to buy them. A Demetrios video is a must-have for any home with a VCR. It doesn't matter if a marrying bride lives there.

To order, write to Demetrios Video, Demetrios for Ilissa, 222 West 37th Street, New York, NY 10018.

Demetrios holds forth in a garment-center office notable not just for its giant L-shaped table of a desk and its madly ringing phones, but also for the vast number of women, all of them smiling, working there. To a visitor, their behavior seems remarkable—all that smiling, in an office? Demetrios is putting out a magazine: *The Bride by Demetrios* (400 pages, twice a year, $4.95 on newsstands); Demetrios is producing a video, *Demetrios* (60 gowns, 45 minutes, $9.95); Demetrios is opening a package of toddler clothing for his children that his mother just sent up from Florida; Demetrios is conducting an interview with a reporter; Demetrios is ordering lunch. And everyone is smiling.

"I am here to answer a fairy tale," he says.

Okay. But if he couldn't design, manufacture, distribute, and promote bridal gowns, many of which sell more than five thousand pieces a year; and if he couldn't just take off and cruise the Mediterranean, either—if he had to work, but not at this—what would he do? He'd be a psychiatrist, he imagines, leading journeys out of fantasy rather than into it. As it is, however, he's enormously successful at what he does, and very happy.

And why not? He's fulfilled his *own* fantasy.

As Demetrios puts it, "I make a gown the people like."

DRESSING THE PART

The Goods on the Gowns

All wedding gowns are not created the same. (Neither are they priced the same, but that's only a related matter.) Selective brides embrace the gauzy chic of a Pat Kerr, the elegant understatement of a Dior, the dazzling beads of an Ilissa. They understand that while there may be millions of bridal gowns out there, only some are the best. These are the dresses that take the bride down the aisle on transports of rapture. Put another way, almost anyone can come up with a white dress. But a few manufacturers consistently deliver the goods.

High End

1 CHRISTIAN DIOR. *601 Davisville Road, Willow Grove, PA 19090.* Price range: $2,200–$4,000. No clutter, great design, impeccable construction. Generally, just kind of European and swell.

2 CAROLINA HERRERA. *48 West 38th Street, New York, NY 10018.* Price range: $2,500–$6,000. Emphasis on classic looks with full skirts and fitted bodices. Designer Herrera ("I don't like these very sexy gowns with décolletage and masses of embroidery") shuns the ornate and the beaded.

3 PAT KERR INC. *200 Wagner Place, Memphis, TN 38103.* Price range: $2,500–$20,000. Designs fashioned from antique lace and other generally diaphanous materials. Sheer beauty (pun intended). If you wish to phone the manufacturer, simply dial (901) 525-LACE.

PHOTO COURTESY CAROLINA HERRERA COUTURE BRIDAL COLLECTION

4 SCAASI BRIDE. *Eva Haynal Forsyth Enterprises, 1385 Broadway, New York, NY 10018.* Price range: $2,300–$5,000. Remember when Kerry Kennedy wed Andrew Cuomo? That was a Scaasi dress she was wearing. The famed society designer may spell his name backward, but he gets his bridal gowns right. One hundred percent silk, detailed handwork, regal designs—and such occasional departures as the micro-mini with the feather hem that was all the rage among professional women last season.

Affordable, More or Less

1 AMSALE. *347 W. 39th Street, Room 11N, New York, NY 10018.* Price range: $1,350–$10,000+. Dresses conceived in dignity: sleek and simple and breathtaking. Many are custom-made. Average cost of an Amsale gown is $1,800.

2 BIANCHI. *293 A Street, Boston, MA 02210.* Price range: $800–$3,500. At the top of the line, they use considerable imported Lyons lace. Special attention to bodice and sleeves; maybe they don't get insane about the skirt.

3 BRIDAL ORIGINALS. *P.O. Box 749, Collinsville, IL 62234.* Price range: $450–$1,200. Embroidery plus miles of satin. Bridal Originals is noted for offering gowns in every size, from petite to size 30.

4 CHRISTOS. *241 West 37th Street, New York, NY 10018.* Price range: $1,000–$5,000. The Baroque look in white silk satin with re-embroidered beaded lace and other lavish embellishments.

5 DEMETRIOS FOR ILISSA. *222 West 37th Street, New York, NY 10018.* Price range: $500–$6,000. Completely out of control. Satin, beads, lace, embroidery—the works. Ilissa isn't just a dress, it's a state of mind. Buy the magazine! Write for the video!

6 THE DIAMOND COLLECTION. *1385 Broadway, New York, NY 10018.* Price range: $1,000–$4,000. Contemporary dresses for contemporary American brides. These designs are apt to look and function more like ball gowns than like costumes for a princess; in fact, for the bride on the party and/or benefit circuit, several are rewearable.

7 EVE OF MILADY. *1375 Broadway, New York, NY 10018.* Price range: $900–$4,000. A dizzying proliferation of designs featuring big skirts, big sleeves, big headpieces. An Eve of Milady dress is a lot to manage, but they say the weight is redistributed when you're wearing it.

8 GALINA. *498 Seventh Avenue, New York, NY 10018.* Price range: $700–$3,000. Updated classics—traditional with a twist. Bouffant skirts and a tendency toward short, puffy sleeves. Daring use of blush pink. Really pretty.

9 JIM HJELM/A PRIVATE COLLECTION. *1375 Broadway, New York, NY 10018.* Price range: $1,500–$3,000. Dramatic dresses distinguished by imaginative use of silk, taffeta, and other luxurious fabrics. The witty ensemble worn by Molly Ringwald as the bride in the movie *Betsy's Wedding* was by Jim Hjelm.

10 PRISCILLA OF BOSTON. *40 Cambridge Street, Charlestown, MA 02129.* Price range: manufacturer declines to disclose. Incredibly refined and understated dresses. If the Pilgrims had lived later and been only slightly less restrained they could have had fun weddings and worn Priscilla gowns.

11 PAULA VARSALONA. *1375 Broadway, New York, NY 10018.* Price range: $1,000–$10,000. She designed the gown worn by the bride in the 1989 Rose Bowl Parade ceremony listed by the *Guinness Book of World Records* as the "World's Most Witnessed Wedding." Such details as hand-rolled organdy flowers or alençon lace abound, usually on a dress fitted to emphasize the female figure.

PHOTO COURTESY JIM HJELM/A PRIVATE COLLECTION

MODEL: LEAH JENSEN, WILHELMINA MODELS, NEW YORK. PHOTO: MEMO ZACK, NEW YORK, FOR PAULA VARSALONA

1 ALFRED ANGELO. *601 Davisville Road, Willow Grove, PA 19090.* Price range: $195–$700. The dream maker. Lots of satin and beads. All the manufacturing is done domestically; the company is proud of creating American jobs.

2 BONNY. *2669 Saturn Street, Brea, CA 92621.* Price range: manufacturer declines to disclose. Satin, beads, lace, huge sleeves—often all on one dress. The home of the peek-a-boo neckline.

3 COUNTRY ELEGANCE. *7353 Greenbush Avenue, North Hollywood, CA 91605.* Price range: $400–$700. Look for the ad with the line of poetry from Emily Dickinson, whose name is misspelled. The ethereal look, largely. Chiffon, lace, patchwork satin are typical fabrics.

4 LILI BY ORYONI. *Bridal Merchandising Concepts, 1117 East Main Street, Alhambra, CA 91801.* Price range: $200–$600. Satin, and they don't skimp on the beaded appliqué work. Comparable to the Ilissa budget line.

124

5 J.C. PENNEY. *For catalogue request and toll-free ordering: 1-800-527-8345.* Penney offers some excellent wedding dresses in satin and lace for under $400; others in lace or taffeta for under $300; still others for under $200. You can charge, and they'll deliver to your home or office. You're on your own with alterations.

6 T.C. ORIGINALS. *P.O. Box 445, La Puente, CA 91747.* Price range: manufacturer declines to disclose. Dresses

PHOTOS COURTESY SUSAN LANE AND COUNTRY ELEGANCE

PHOTO COURTESY LILI BY ORYONI

are often decorated with ruffles, bows, swags, fabric flowers; the effect is vaguely antebellum.

Rule of Thumb: A bridal gown appearing by itself in a full-page color ad in Bride's or Modern Bride probably retails anywhere from $1,200 to $2,000 +; gowns shown three to a page are more likely to be in the $400–$600 range.

THE ARGUMENTS FOR RENTING YOUR BRIDAL GOWN

- A gown is an expense.
- Why spend good money on something you'll wear only once.
- If you're in New York or Los Angeles, it's easy.*

* Try: Just Once, Ltd., 292 Fifth Avenue, New York, NY 10001 (212-465-0960); Dressed to Kill, 8762 Holloway Drive, West Hollywood, CA 90069 (213-652-4334)

THE ARGUMENTS AGAINST RENTING YOUR BRIDAL GOWN

- You can't do alterations on a rental.
- The bride who wore it previously may not have taken care of it at a boisterous reception. In fact, she may have stained it.
- There are very nice low-priced dresses you can buy instead.
- You're not going to feel special in it, and if you don't feel special you won't look special, and if you don't look special the pictures will show it, and you want to look your best in the pictures because they're going to be around forever.

OTHER THINGS
YOU COULD BUY
FOR ROUGHLY $5,000
INSTEAD OF A COUTURE
WEDDING GOWN

• A CAR. The new 1991 Hyundai Excel, with fuel injection, front-wheel drive, steel-belted all-season Goodyear radial tires, five-mile-per-hour bumpers, bodyside molding, deluxe hubcaps, dual mirrors, fully reclining bucket seats, intermittent wipers, and front and rear defrosters, was discounted in various parts of the country to $5,759.

• A SEMESTER AT DARTMOUTH. In 1991, tuition for a semester at this college, which is on the trimester system, cost $5,089.

• ROOM AND BOARD FOR A YEAR AT HARVARD. Eating and sleeping in the house system during the academic year 1990–91 cost $5,125.

• A MINK COAT. If you're comfortable wearing animal skins, the Burlington Coat Factory in New York discounted female mink coats in 1991 to as low as $1,499.

• CLOTHES FOR THE GROOM. A Savile Row suit such as the kind worn by Tom Hanks in *Bonfire of the Vanities* features the broad-shouldered, slim-hipped, tapered-waist look. British tailor Henry Stewart's suits are handmade, use $200-a-yard worsted wool, and retailed at $4,000 in 1990.

• A TRIP TO PARIS. From New York's Kennedy Airport to the Charles de Gaulle Airport in Paris is $3,194 on the Concorde.

• A WHOLE LOT OF FUNDING FOR YOUR CAUSE, CAMPAIGN, OR CANDIDATE.

IF I WERE A SEAMSTRESS, WOULD YOU MARRY ME ANYWAY?

Analyzing the Patterns

 here are several reasons people sew: to save money, relax, express themselves, punish themselves. And there are several reasons brides sew their own bridal gowns: because it's such a beautiful tradition; because you can use fabrics and trimmings you'd never be able to find except on your own; because you want to make a fashion statement and/or wear an exclusive; because you're a professional costume designer. Should you elect to start from scratch, be aware of the following:

PATTERNS FOR BRIDAL GOWNS ARE HARD. Vogue, the couture pattern maker that likes to throw around French phrases, labels its bridal styles *très difficile*. If you've ever had trouble fitting sleeves, working with linings, or sewing delicate fabric, think twice (and steer clear of chiffon no matter what): there may come a moment when pushing voluminous skirts through the machine seems more like sailmaking than fun.

ALL THE MAJOR PATTERN MAKERS OFFER BRIDAL STYLES. Check the "Bridal" section in the regular, seasonal pattern book and you'll find designs influenced by the gowns currently most popular at retail. New Look has patterns for $4.00 (one charming bridal gown comes with a miniature version for a flower girl); Simplicity patterns are $5.95 and $6.95; McCall's, $9.50; Vogue, $15.00. Most also offer patterns for accessories (it takes about 3¼ yards of 108-inch-wide tulle, netting, or illusion to make a headpiece with a short veil).

SOME SPECIALTY MAIL ORDER COMPANIES OFFER PATTERNS. For historic designs from 1830 to 1939, try Past Patterns, 2017 Eastern, S.E., Grand Rapids, MI 49507 (616) 245-9456. For folk styles, try Ethnic Accessories, Box 250, Forestville, CA 95436.

MOST BRIDAL GOWNS TAKE ABOUT 13¾ YARDS OF MATERIAL. Pattern books suggest such fabrics as cotton, lawn, taffeta, crepe, silk, raw silk, satin. Figure on using more fabric for a winter wedding than for a summer ceremony. And you may want to embellish with seed pearls, lace, other trimmings. YOU CAN MAKE PETTICOATS BY REUSING THE PATTERN PIECES FOR THE SKIRT. Don't forget that your dress will look infinitely better if it falls the way it's supposed to; make a full skirt flare out by putting it over an undergarment made from muslin or a stiff synthetic. PATTERNS FOR BALL GOWNS CAN BE ADAPTED TO BRIDAL GOWNS AND BRIDESMAIDS' DRESSES. McCall's has a particularly pretty array of basic dance dresses. (Check the lingerie section of the pattern book too. There might be a design there that could make up as a sensational wedding dress if you use the right fabric.)

WHY STEPHANOTIS? WHITHER ORANGE BLOSSOMS?

Choosing Your Bouquet

 trip to your florist should produce the wedding album distributed nationwide by the American Floral Service. Inside are scores of full-color photos of bridal bouquets in the $35–$225 price range. (Each lavish construction is captioned with a phrase such as "contemporary refinement," or "genteel style," or "quiet sophistication" that might as easily apply to a model home as to a bride's bouquet, but that's another matter.) The American bride's favorite flower, the stephanotis, is everywhere in these pictures, as are lily-of-the-valley, roses, orchids, chrysanthemums. There are so many varieties of flowers, in fact, that it's possible to order an asters-and-eucalyptus creation, not to mention the "eccentric bridal masterpiece" of orchids, lily buds, and dried pods.

But nowhere is there the orange blossom. Nor is your florist likely to recommend it. Or the magazines to picture it. It just didn't make it in North America. Still, it's the flower the stephanotis is mimicking. Originally, the orange blossom, which is white, not orange, and looks as pure as the driven snow but is from a tree that is wildly, almost embarrassingly, fruitful, was associated with the Virgin Mary and used in Renaissance religious art to connote innocence. Today, stephanotis has taken over. The stephanotis resembles the orange blossom and so it has come to mean purity. Talk with your florist about carrying something charming—a cascade, a sweep, a nosegay, a tussy mussy—on your wedding day. And, if you think of it, mourn the orange blossom as you would your virginity.

Nothing can drive up the cost of a wedding faster than flowers. So, gather ye rosebuds where ye may—but try daisies too—they're less expensive. Or omit the bouquet altogether.

**SOME THINGS BRIDES
CHOOSE TO CARRY INSTEAD
OF A BOUQUET**
COVERED BIBLE
FUR MUFF
ANTIQUE FAN
SINGLE PERFECT BLOSSOM

Many brides have asked: If stephanotis means purity, what do the other flowers mean? The key:

Aster • daintiness
Pink carnation • I'll never forget you
Daffodil • regard
Daisy • loyal love, innocence
Gardenia • secret love, joy
Heather • admiration
Ivy • affection, fidelity
Calla lily • beauty
Lily-of-the-valley • sweetness, happiness
Orchid • many children
Rose • love
Pink rose • perfect happiness
White rose • I am worthy of you
Blue violet • fidelity, modesty
White violet • Let's take a chance

NOTE: Stay away from yellow roses unless for some reason you're trying to express jealousy.

129

Slightly cascading bouquet of white dendrobium orchids, wax flower, and Queen Anne's lace, with highlights of pink anemones.

TIMOTHY LEE

Warning: Bridesmaids' dresses stay in the closet long after they're worn, and can show up in random bridesmaid testing at the office, should everyone start laughing about the weddings they've been in and agree to compare their outfits. Among these colleagues, good sports all, evidence of one-time use is conclusive. *Left to right:*

THE LITTLE SLIP OF A THING. Is it a long teddy or a mini-dress? Hard to tell—but it sure is lacy, and with the floral miner's hat to top it off, so cute you could giggle.

THE YOU-ABSOLUTELY-CAN-WEAR-THIS-THING-AGAIN. What could be bad? It's go-anywhere black velvet with a removable white sash that in real life allowed its wearer to lasso a dance partner at the reception.

THE MEXICAN PEASANT. A favorite of theme weddings, other list-toppers include the Hawaiian sarong for the luau wedding, and the gingham jumper for the nuptial hayride.

THE SUPERWOMAN. Don't look now but the detachable gold lamé skirt also becomes a cape!

GARDEN VARIETY. Mad floral print suitable for pre-teens—exhale and the left shoulder drops. (May come with fancy, freesia-covered, Kentucky Derby–style hat.)

THE MERMAID. This dress slows the procession because you have to mince down the aisle—but if you ever need an Elvira, Mistress of the Night, costume, or a sexy get-up for New Year's Eve, you're set.

THE ACETATE HORROR. It's not just the dyed-to-contrast pumps that pinch to death—anywhere near a lighted match you're in danger of going up in flames.

THE SHARPER IMAGE

Correct Attire for the Groom and His Men

 ou'll read that color is all the rage, but don't believe it for a minute—except, perhaps, where the Pocket Square (fancy handkerchief) is concerned. The groom's clothing should be a controlled foil for the bride's finery. She's dazzling; he's dashing. Natural good looks and a trim physique help, but not as much as a skilled haberdasher or reliable rental place. *Basic guidelines:* A very formal wedding before six in the evening means a cutaway and striped trousers; after six, white tie, black tails, satin-trimmed trousers. A formal evening wedding means a black or gray stroller with striped trousers. Semiformal or informal daytime equals a dark suit. Ring bearers wear short pants and knee-highs. Fathers dress like the wedding party. *Basic tips:* Be measured for your outfits about three months before the wedding and pick up your suits about three days ahead of time. *Try on everything before leaving the store.* The best man returns the groom's suit the first business day after the wedding; ushers return their own suits. In every sense of the word, it's distinguishing that you all look alike.

The Sartorial Options Demystified

TUXEDO. You can have it single- or double-breasted and there's an area of choice surrounding the lapels, which can have little points, or notches, or be just standard wraparound.

WHITE TIE. It goes with a stiff white shirt, white vest, and black tails.

CUTAWAY. Tails for daytime. Wear this coat with striped trousers and an ascot (which the ring bearer will call a mascot).

STROLLER. Like a regular suit jacket but longer. You stroll down the aisle in it.

LAYDOWN COLLAR. The kind you wear to the office.

WING COLLAR. What they wear at the Academy Awards and benefit dances and high school proms: it stands up of its own accord, but the tips fold down, and look like wings.

VEST. Means you won't wear a cummerbund.

CUMMERBUND. It hides your waistband if you're not wearing a vest—and speaking of high school proms? You had one in plaid.

Cutaway with vest, wing-collar, and ascot.

132

BOW TIE. You can wear creative red, or creative floral, or creative anything, but black is preferred.

ASCOT. Involves a stickpin. You gotta really love your bride.

STUDS. Rude jokes aside, it turns out the main use for studs is to take the place of buttons. If you can't figure out how to make them work with your shirt, ask someone.

CUFF LINKS. They link your cuffs and they're favorite gift items for groomsmen. Act grateful. You need them. (Otherwise you'd have to use buttons!)

BOUTONNIERE. The flower you wear on your left lapel as a kind of grace note to the symphony of your look. It's usually a flower the bride is carrying in her bouquet, too.

POCKET SQUARE. The fancy handkerchief. Don't blow your nose in it.

ccording to *New York Times* fashion writer Carrie
Donovan, female guests attending a large afternoon
or early evening wedding should wear: a short dress
or suit. They should not wear: anything strapless,
pants if they can help it, solid black (prints are better), or all-white.

Quiz 2

IN THE ROYAL STYLE

The bride is the most beautiful woman on earth. She gets that way by
making the crucial decisions that give her whatever look she desires—
country girl, pouting debutante, wispy muse, other. For her, finding the
right wedding dress is no harder than finding the right groom. That's
because she knows herself—and has the correct information. Test yourself below. Answers at the bottom.

1 Taffeta and tulle are:
   (a) exotic dancers scheduled for the bachelor party
   (b) fabrics
   (c) types of lace

2 Chantilly and Venise refer to:
   (a) cities in France and Italy that might be right for your honeymoon
   (b) floral designs worked in lace
   (c) songs about women and boatmen

3 Bishop and dolman are:
   (a) chess pieces
   (b) officiants at the wedding of a bridal couple from different religious
   backgrounds
   (c) types of sleeves (hint: bishop is a full sleeve gathered into a wide
   cuff at wrist; dolman extends from a large armhole in a capelike
   effect)

4 Queen Anne is:
(a) a former monarch and probably a very nice woman
(b) a kind of lacy-looking flower that some people are allergic to
(c) a neckline that's so high in the back it almost forms a collar, but so low in the front you could almost call it plunging

5 The princess line is:
(a) a cruise ship
(b) what you're giving people now that you're a bride
(c) the kind of waist fitted with vertical seams instead of a waistband, a feature of many especially slimming wedding dresses

Answers: 1.b; 2.b; 3.c; 4.c; 5.c

Putting It All in Perspective 2

• The average age of the American bride rose during the past decade—to twenty-four.
• In much of Asia and throughout Islam, the bride is kept in seclusion for days or weeks before the ceremony, and is carried in a hooded palanquin to arrive, swathed in veils, before her husband.
• Anne of Brittany was the first noted bride in modern history to dress all in white for her wedding, in 1498, to Louis XII of France.
• Nellie Custis, Martha Washington's granddaughter, may have influenced the American preference for a lacy white bridal veil. At her own wedding, she wore a long scarf that was a reference to a fond moment: her groom, glimpsing her through a lace curtain at an open window, had complimented her.
• Empress Eugénie wore an orange-blossom wreath at her 1853 marriage to Napoleon.
• In the 1920s in the south of France it was briefly all the rage for brides to be married wearing lounging pajamas.
• At Mick Jagger's first wedding, to Bianca Jagger (in the sixties), the bride arrived for her marriage nude and on horseback.
• Finnish brides used to cut their hair short on their wedding day and never show it again.
• In 1989, the average cost of a wedding dress was $794, not including the veil, which cost about $170.
• *Milwaukee-talkie:* Three Wisconsin brides, former school chums, were the subject of conversation when, in 1930, they sewed one wedding dress to share at a trio of weddings held the same summer.
• Vera Wang, of the Wang computer family, was design director for Ralph Lauren before opening Vera Wang Bridal House in Manhattan.
• At her 1986 wedding to Swiss shipping tycoon Arne Naess, singer Diana Ross wore a Bob Mackie gown that reportedly cost $50,000.

• In 1990, California bridal designer Susan Lane made four "eco dresses." Each dress represented and contained elements from four recyclable product categories—glass, aluminum, plastic, and paper.

Glass

Aluminum

Paper

Plastic

• A bridesmaid spends an average of $149 on her dress.

• In 1991, *The New York Times Magazine* pictured contemporary brides outfitted in ruffled pants of royal blue and short-short dresses of marigold and fuschia.

• According to a *Bride's* magazine poll, 94 percent of brides have formal weddings, at which 64 percent of the grooms wear tuxedos. Ninety-seven percent of the grooms reported their brides had decided what they wore.

• Says *Glamour* magazine, the most popular bridal hemline is floor length with chapel train; most popular neckline is sweetheart; most popular fabric is satin; most popular headpiece is floral wreath.

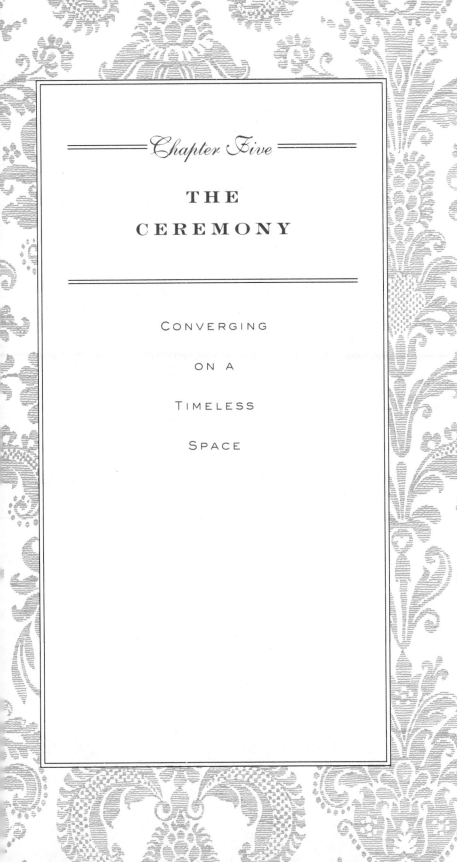

Chapter Five

THE
CEREMONY

CONVERGING

ON A

TIMELESS

SPACE

SAY WHEN

Selecting the Month, Day, and Hour of the Ceremony

our thoughts on the most propitious time for your wedding may well come down to the exact minute your astrologer advises or the exact weekend the reception hall is available. Whatever, most people don't get married in January (the big wedding months are June, August, September, and December); the most popular day is June 30; the odds are you'll marry on either Saturday or Sunday; and the favorite hours for the ceremony sound like a cheer: two, four, six, eight. Your choice of an afternoon or evening wedding will influence everything from the dress you wear (heavy beads under a high sun are doubtless a bit much) to the food you serve (the guests may expect dinner). Rule of thumb: the earlier in the day the wedding takes place, the less expensive it is. Because of the Christian belief that Jesus ascended to heaven at dawn, the church has long preferred a morning wedding. However, before the time of Christ, grooms often went to their brides in the dark, the origin of the evening wedding. Choose as you will. Pick a time, pencil it in. We'll see you there, with bells on. Meanwhile, some helpful verse:

> *Monday for wealth,*
> *Tuesday for health,*
> *Wednesday the best day of all;*
> *Thursday for crosses,*
> *Friday for losses,*
> *Saturday no luck at all.*
> —Nineteenth-century English refrain

> *June means weddings in everyone's lexicon,*
> *Weddings in Swedish, weddings in Mexican*
> *Breezes play Mendelssohn, treeses play Youmans,*
> *Birds wed birds, and humans wed humans*
> *All year long the gentlemen woo,*
> *But the ladies dream of a June "I do."*
> *Ladies grow loony, and gentlemen loonier;*
> *This year's June is next year's Junior.*
> —"Here Usually Comes the Bride," by Ogden Nash

The License

here are certain activities in this country for which a citizen needs a license; however, requirements for the wedding license vary from state to state. Call your marriage bureau or county clerk's office at least one month before the wedding to find out what you're supposed to do and how much the fee is, but don't actually go for the license until closer to your wedding day. Briefly, many states insist on:

• A blood test (New York, Louisiana, Illinois, Nevada don't; most others do. *Note:* Georgia requires a rubella test; California requires it for women under fifty)
• Proof of identity (birth certificate, passport, driver's license, or military ID = usually okay)
• Proof of parental consent (if you're really young—ask, if you're not yet twenty-three)
• Proof of divorce (if you were married before, obviously) or the date and place the divorce or annulment became final

Be sure to inquire about restrictions. Usually the license is valid throughout the state, but sometimes it must be used in the county where it was obtained. Often there's a short "cooling off" period, but usually the license is good for at least thirty days.

he instant everything changes in the bridal couple's life is likely to be the very moment they wish to express their sense of continuity. Bridal couples who do not choose to marry in church or at a temple may nevertheless begin thinking about tradition and historic weightiness. (As location-finding expert Hannelore Hahn puts it, "Every bride wants a mansion with a view.") There are many, many, *many* wonderful places to marry: at a city registry, the club, the beach; on a boat, ship, ferry, or aircraft carrier; in a garden, loft, or brownstone; at a gallery, on a mountaintop, in a hotel, at home. Make sure there are both indoor and outdoor accommodations, in case of rain, and then let your imagination run. The following is a nationwide roundup of choice situations. At each, a reception for 150 guests can immediately follow the ceremony.

140

Top Eight

1 HAMMERSMITH FARM, *Ocean Drive, Newport, RI 02840 (401) 846-7346.* This is where Jackie Kennedy and the future President had their wedding reception, in 1953; if not the absolute best place in the world, it must surely have been the original Camelot. To call it a farm raises understatement to new heights: its twenty-eight rooms overlook the yachts on Narragansett Bay

and its gardens were landscaped by Frederick Law Olmstead (who also did a little something in New York called Central Park). You can get married here April–October; write or call Linda Michaud one year to six months ahead to discuss the fee, to reserve, and to get a list of suggested caterers, suppliers, accommodations for your guests. Hotels and motels, by the way, are in historic Newport, where Dennis Connor trained for the America's Cup and Claus von Bülow did or did not inject his wife with insulin.

2 LEONARD'S OF GREAT NECK, *555 Northern Boulevard, Great Neck, Long Island, NY 11021 (516) 487-7900.* Free yarmulkes, twelve banquet rooms, and chapels too. The undisputed, hands-down winner among the huge catering halls. Look at it this way: if you get tired of your own wedding, you can always slip next door to someone else's. Book one year in advance.

3 THE QUEEN MARY, P.O. Box 8, Pier J, Long Beach, CA 90801 (213) 435-5671. She crossed the Atlantic 1,001 times, but she's a floating 400-room hotel now, and will accept as many as 1,500 people for your wedding in Los Angeles Harbor. (As if that weren't enough, Howard Hughes's *Spruce Goose*, the largest wooden flying boat and boondoggle ever built, is next door.) Write or call Banquet Sales one year in advance (Saturday evenings are snapped up early) to get on board. Estimated cost for an evening wedding with 150 guests: $6,500–$7,000, including dinner and bar. Bring your own musicians.

PHOTO COURTESY THE QUEEN MARY

4 THE RAINBOW ROOM, *30 Rockefeller Center, New York, NY 10020 (212) 632-5100.* Society's favorite, on top of New York, the cherry on the sundae. Michael Jackson, Liza Minnelli, Lee Iacocca, the Duchess of York party here. It's extraordinarily expensive (management won't even begin to say how much, it's so individual and all), but you knew that. You can bring in your own band, music, flowers, et cetera, or they'll do everything for you. The suites on the sixty-fourth and sixty-fifth floors are available anytime, but the Rainbow Room itself can be used for weddings only on Saturday and Sunday afternoons and Sunday and Monday evenings. Ideal number of guests for the room is 175 to

250, but if you have less they'll make it seem like more. Never too early to book, of course (call Tony Zazula), but give them at least eight months to get ready for you. And have fun.

5 SOUTH FORK RANCH, *P.O. Box 863773, Plana, TX 75086 (214) 442-6536.* Yes! It's *the* ranch, the site of all the outdoor scenes on the TV series "Dallas." That it's also the number-one tourist attraction in Texas shouldn't deter you: book nine months to one year in advance and you can make the mansion yours. Figure approximately $7,500 for a stand-up reception with cocktails and hors d'oeuvres for 150 guests. If you want a rodeo too, it will run you $2,500–$3,000 extra.

6 THE PHILADELPHIA ZOO, *34th and Girard Avenues, Philadelphia, PA 19104 (215) 387-6400.* A fee of approximately $1,200 will get you the Tree House or the Rare Animal House, and you can tie the knot while a lot of primates, including chimps and gorillas, look on. There's an exclusive caterer, Gordon Keith, who will help with food, drink, the menu for a seated dinner of 120 people (or a cocktail reception for as many as 220)—and negotiate according to your needs. He has band referrals too, or you can bring in your own. Reserve nine months to one year in advance.

7 FAIR LANE, *The University of Michigan/Dearborn, 4901 Evergreen Road, Dearborn, MI 48128 (313) 593-5590.* Henry Ford's estate, named for the road his father was born on in Ireland. For Michigan graduates, the site makes better sense than Dooley's or the Liberty Bell, in Ann Arbor—and for anyone who's ever driven a Ford Fairlane, it's sheer poetry. A baronial mansion that's yours for a fee dependent on the number of rooms you require.

8 THE GRAIN EXCHANGE ROOM, *Mackie Building, 225 East Michigan Street, Milwaukee, WI 53202 (414) 276-7840.* A 60′ x 115′ hall that until 1910 was the largest cash grain market in the world. It's lavishly decorated with marble murals, frescoes, friezes, gold leaf, stained glass, columns, a skylight. You can have it for $150 per hour, with a four-hour minimum Sunday through Friday, and an eight-hour minimum on Saturday. They'll give you a list of recommended caterers or you can bring in your own. Call Eileen, the Event Coordinator, eighteen months to one year in advance.

TENT RENT

enting a tent amounts to putting a reception hall in the backyard. The first thing to consider is whether the yard can handle this. For a wedding for 150 people, anywhere from 2,500 to 3,000 square feet will be required. The tent renters can work around the odd stately oak or two, and they can actually construct *over* the 6-foot hedge, but they do need their space. Your space. Which brings us to the second thing to consider: whether you can handle this. Renting a tent means (among other things) that a crew of four or five workmen will be on the premises for four to eight hours both the day before the wedding and the day after, and that in between—well, there will be 150 people out there.

Brides who rent tents are often like women who love too much: they trust rather easily. Instead, caution should be taken. Thinking of the tent as both chapel and reception hall, reserve yours as early as a year in advance (leave a deposit, get a contract) in order to avoid the rush at the height of the season. Ask the purveyor if he's a member of the Tent Renters Division of Industrial Fabrics International, and if he's not, be very wary. A state-of-the-art tent for 150 people should rent, on a flat fee, for about $1,600–$1,800. It should be able to withstand winds of fifty to sixty miles per hour, and even be able to get through an eighty-mile-an-hour hurricane (and undoubtedly memorable wedding). It should be made of durable material and come with sidewalls to keep out rain and wind. It should be able to accommodate heating ducts from a unit outside the tent, and be capable of being rigged for lighting (usually about $200 extra). It should have 4- to 5-foot stakes to anchor it; disaster stories about tents usually center on their blowing away. Buyer beware if you're being promised a lot for as little as $500. Check out such things as the quality of the fabric—lightweight "do-it-yourself" structures leak.

Recent breakthroughs in vinyl have allowed the sparkling all-white tent to triumph. Favored by brides, it replaces not only the more dated yellow-, blue-, or pink-and-white striped models of yesteryear, but also those all-white canvas structures that were always getting dirty and didn't look much better than old sneakers. A vinyl tent is easily cleaned between uses (so see to it that yours has been). Thus it looms pristine, outside the kitchen window, like a cloud bank, or drifting snow, or a giant marshmallow.

Or something. Supply your own analogy, this is your wedding. Just remember that tent renting is a service profession and that backing the truck over the lawn and leaving deep ruts should come neither with the territory nor on it. Someone tell those guys to take it easy. *You* tell those guys to take it easy. Maybe this wasn't such a great idea—maybe if you wanted a tent you should have joined the Girl Scouts. . . .

But no, wait—look what's happening out there! An oasis, a fairyland, heaven. Hang on to your fantasies! Hang on to the sidewalls! It's everything you've been looking for.

Right in your own backyard.

WOMEN OF THE IVY LEAGUE, UNITE!

ow that most universities have admitted women, so have their alumni clubs. These former bastions of old-boyism are pretty places for your wedding. They offer all the charm of a Founders Hall—they're apt to have wooden walls, high ceilings, marble floors— and all the personal comfort of a friend's living room. In Manhattan, where alumni groups from Harvard, Yale, and Princeton all have clubs with banquet facilities; where alumni from Cornell are constructing a veritable skyscraper; where alumni from Brown can use Princeton's space; and where a variety of other arrangements prevail as well, the possibilities seem endless for the graduate bride of a co-ed college.

Likewise in other parts of the country—often because of the University Club. This organization, founded a century ago, is open to the graduate of any accredited college who is sponsored by a current member. The University Club doesn't advertise its facilities because it doesn't solicit business. Finding it shouldn't be too hard, though: simply ask around or look in the phone book. To have your wedding at a University Club, join, or convince a member to allow you to charge your bill to her account. A ceremony followed by a seated dinner for a hundred runs from $70–$150 a person at most University Clubs. Book three months to one year in advance.

PHONE NUMBERS FOR COLLEGE GRADUATES
Brown University Club in New York Inc. (212) 629-6002
Harvard Club of New York City (212) 840-6600
Princeton Club of New York (212) 840-6400
Yale Club (212) 661-2070
University Club of Los Angeles (213) 627-8651
University Club of San Francisco (415) 781-0900
University Club of Washington, D.C. (202) 862-8800

MARRIAGE'S FIFTH DIMENSION

 n New Jersey, anyone can be a minister. Thus it is that there are several pilot/ministers on the staff of the Air Pirate Balloon Academy in Bedminster. These chaplains of festival flights have performed easily a dozen perfectly legal and binding marriages in and around hot-air balloons. "The bride has usually been married before," explains director Jack Grenton. "She's finished with the floppy hats and the bridesmaids. She's looking for some adventure."

DRAWBACKS OF A BALLOON WEDDING. You have to get up extremely early, and so do your guests. The Air Pirates are aloft at dawn, so you invite everyone to this specific meadow and they watch either as you get married and then step in the basket or as you step in the basket and then get married, in the air.

PLUSES OF A BALLOON WEDDING. It's completely uplifting. Maybe you've never been on a plane before, let alone this thing, and yet here you are floating through the air. Everyone waves. If your mother in Oregon couldn't make it, she can be hooked up to the ceremony via cellular phone, and down on the ground your guests can hear your words too, because they're amplified over a loudspeaker.

THE SLIGHT ANXIETY OF A BALLOON WEDDING.

You don't know where you're going to come down. However, the chase balloon carrying the videographer is getting everything on tape, including your whereabouts. When you do land you'll be driven back to the Ryland Inn for a wedding breakfast where mimosas flow like water. Says Grenton, launching yourself into a sea of air with no firm idea of what's going to happen next is just like being married. No point in worrying, then. Trust, and celebrate!

Air Pirate Balloon Academy, Lamington Road, Bedminster, NJ 07921 (800) 4 HOT AIR. Basic cost: $1,000 for garlanded wedding balloon carrying bridal couple and two attendants on one-hour flight. Additional guests in chase balloon: $195 per person. Breakfast at the Ryland Inn: approximately $20 a head. The Academy will also issue press releases for a negotiated fee.

A NEAT IDEA

The Military Wedding

 ou can be married in a military wedding if either you or your intended is on active duty, a reservist, or retired from the service; all you have to do to make your wedding military is have it in a military chapel or wear your uniform in a civilian setting. *Answer to the most frequently asked question: No!* You are not required to obtain permission from your command to have your wedding. A wedding is not a military function. *Exception to the rule:* If there's a published order with specific instructions in your unit, it takes precedence and you must disregard the above. *Examples:* Students enrolled at the Naval Academy at Annapolis are prohibited from marrying in any sort of wedding, military or otherwise, before graduation. Likewise prohibited from marrying: marine guards and security officers stationed at foreign embassies.

Choosing a chaplain is linked to choosing the marriage site. If you're on a base and using its chapel, no problem; the chaplain will perform the ceremony. If you're off base, the chance he'll oblige decreases as distance increases. As one active-duty chaplain put it: "I would not go to Hometown USA unless it was close.

People can have a military wedding with their own clergyperson simply by wearing their uniforms." Chaplains will not accept a fee or gratuity, but you can make a donation to the chapel. Chaplains can perform the ceremony of any denomination, or work with you to create your own vows. Finally, chaplains can preside over everything from a supersonic ceremony in the cockpit of an F4 fighter jet to a quieter affair with just the family and the other lance corporals.

The most typical military wedding these days joins an active-duty groom with a civilian bride, but trending fast is the military bride and her military groom. Although her full-dress uniform is perfectly correct attire for the bride (and her bridesmaids may appear in uniform, too), brides at military weddings seem to prefer wearing white, even when they're active-duty personnel. Protocol is relaxed. Strictly speaking, guests should be seated according to rank, but this is hard to achieve when the admiral insists on both appearing in civilian clothes and slipping in unnoticed. Besides, as a Navy chaplain remarked: "At a wedding, moms and dads come first."

If you are asked to be in a military wedding but are not in the military yourself, just wear regular formal attire.

If you are planning a military wedding:

- Include the bride's and groom's rank and service on the invitations.
- Go for the arch of swords at the end of the recessional if you're an officer. The ushers, in uniform, form two lines facing each other; at the command, they raise their swords to form an arch under which the bride and groom pass.

A TRIP TO THE ALBERTSON WEDDING CHAPEL

The Albertson Wedding Chapel, at the corner of Wilshire and La Brea in Los Angeles, is the scene of approximately twelve weddings a week. A friend writes:

You can be married here whether or not you're a Californian (or an American, for that matter)—*if* you are willing to swear you're already living with your intended as a spouse. Alex Garcia, director of the Chapel, cites California Civil Code 4213, when he says, "The law figures if you're living together, it's too late for a blood test."

Stand on the sidewalk across the street from Albertson's and you'll spy the famous HOLLYWOOD sign grinning down from the hills above, magnet for dreamers and fantasists. Inside Albertson's, the surroundings are a bit more pragmatic. The waiting room, with stacks of *Sports Illustrated* and *Elle*, features display cases of bridal headpieces and bouquets for rent; hanging on the walls are framed photos of numerous just-marrieds. Beyond the waiting room is the chapel itself, decorated with stained-glass windows, parquet floors, chandeliers—and fitted out with several rows of pews for guests.

I visited Albertson's on a day when a couple in their twenties came in and spent a few minutes in the waiting room answering questions on a clipboard, almost instantly to become husband and wife. Garcia says couples often have pressing needs—they're pregnant, say, or one partner needs to get on the other's medical plan at work, or the INS is getting sticky about the Green Card. For all that, the two consenting adults at Albertson's the day I was there looked entirely romantic.

Important information: You can wear your own bridal gown and tux or rent Albertson's. You can request a civil, religious, or non-denominational ceremony. The cost of the basic no-frills package for a couple age eighteen or older and living together is $175; this includes the wedding license, the filing fee, the use of the chapel, and the minister's services. The chapel is open seven days a week. Elizabeth Taylor's son married J. P. Getty's granddaughter here. If speed is an issue, ask for the "Lunch Hour Wedding." *Albertson Wedding Chapel, 5217 Wilshire Boulevard, Los Angeles, CA 90036 (213) 937-4919.*

GOING TO SCHOOL

Or, How to Find Skilled Musicians

ot since that time you heard the Leningrad Symphony on tour have you seen an audience quite so enthralled—or at least that's the reaction you like to picture when you imagine your guests listening to the music at your wedding. Unfortunately, it is often hard for the bride to know who will perform that music, or even what it is. Keep the following points in mind as you look for those talents who can make a joyful noise at the ceremony:

WORKING A WEDDING IS TO THE SERIOUS MUSICIAN SOMETHING LIKE BABY-SITTING IS TO A PARENT: NOT THE REAL THING. However, the future finest musical performers in the country may in fact be available via a music school in your city. The more famous it is, the less likely it will be to advertise the availability of its students as for-hire soloists and ensembles, of course—but call the placement office and ask anyway. Be obsequious. Be discreet. Be thrilled when they produce the name of a tenor.

THE MUSICIAN HAS EXPERTISE. Perhaps you've ended up with a music teacher at a community music school rather than a student at an urban conservatory. In either case, you are dealing with someone who has chosen to devote his career to the knowledge of music. He knows a lot, so try the best you can to articulate the mood you want at the ceremony, and then listen closely to his suggestions. Many musicians say that bridal couples have exaggerated expectations, which the professional can help pull into line. The key is to be as practical about the music as you would about the food: if you want only ten minutes of music, you can't select a piece that takes twenty minutes to play; if you want only a string quartet, it is unwise to select the theme from a movie that isn't scored for strings. Plan ahead, and allow for rehearsal (the more performers there are, the more time they'll need to coordinate).

MUSICIANS CHARGE A FEE. Negotiate up front, figuring on $50–$75 per hour per player, and understanding that you must pay for all of the time the musicians are engaged, not just when they're actually playing; this includes rehearsal time. As well, certain instruments (the harp, the timpani) require a cartage fee, usually an additional $50–$75. Transportation is generally included in the musician's fee unless there is distance involved, in which case you're responsible for it. Do not tip (would you tip your surgeon?). And do not ask the most insulting thing you can ever ask a musician: "If we give you dinner, will you play longer?"

CLERICAL OKAY. Some churches have restrictions, so if you're bringing in musicians, or making up your own program, make sure the selections have been cleared with the clergyperson or church musical director. This applies even to religious works.

PACING. Work with the musician on this, and listen to his thoughts. Typically, there's a prelude beginning about a half hour before the ceremony, and maybe a solo or two after the bride's mother has been seated. Then comes the processional! Then a solo during the ceremony . . . and finally the recessional! Thus, in sequence, the effect is: triumphant and thankful; excited; reflective; ecstatic. (Or: Up, up, just a teensy bit down, and away!)

THE TYPE OF MUSIC. Some prefer folk music at their wedding; others, jazz or show tunes (consider such beautiful standards as Sheldon Harnick and Jerry Bock's "Sunrise, Sunset" from *Fiddler on the Roof* or Leonard Bernstein's "One Hand, One Heart" from *West Side Story*). But far and away the most frequently chosen music for the ceremony is classical. Talk with the musician about previewing the selections you're contemplating—they are probably available on tape at Tower Records or Sam Goody.

The Wedding Album, *produced by RCA Victor, is available in stores or by phone (800) 221-8180 for $7.98. Other sources of recordings are: The American Guild of Organists (212) 687-9188 in New York and the National Association of Pastoral Musicians (202) 723-5800 in Washington, D.C.*

ELEVEN TOP MUSIC SCHOOLS

To find the conservatories and music schools near you, consult *Musical America's International Directory of the Performing Arts* (it has hundreds of listings, organized by state), or Nancy Uscher's *The Schirmer Guide to Schools of Music and Conservatories Throughout the World* (Macmillan). Or, try phoning your arts council—every state has one. The following is a short list of acclaimed institutions whose students are accomplished talents:

Baltimore

Peabody Institute of The Johns Hopkins University, 1 East Mount Vernon Place, Baltimore, MD 21202 (301) 659-8100. Why Baltimore has always been a musical center, even before you saw The Peabody (that's how the natives refer to it) in the movie *Men Don't Leave*; absolutely top students.

Boston

New England Conservatory, 290 Huntington Avenue, Boston, MA 02115 (617) 262-1120. We're talking about the very first American conservatory (originally founded in 1853, it was modeled after Mendelssohn's Leipzig Conservatorium); it's located right next door to the Boston Symphony, so a lot of its students never get very far in life—geographically speaking, anyway.

Chicago

American Conservatory of Music, 116 South Michigan Avenue, Chicago, IL 60603 (312) 263-4161. So close to the Chicago Symphony Orchestra, the Chicago Lyric Opera, and the Art Institute of Chicago that the students can become great almost by osmosis.

Dallas

American Institute of Musical Studies, 3500 Maple Avenue, LB-22, Dallas, TX 75219-3901 (214) 528-9234. Their motto is "We take students from studio to stage." Maybe they can stop at your wedding on the way.

Los Angeles

University of Southern California School of Music, University Park, Los Angeles, CA 90007 (213) 743-6935. It's right in the center of Los Angeles, which is attractive to talented student musicians who want to crack the film and recording industries.

New Haven

Yale Institute of Sacred Music, 409 Prospect Street, New Haven, CT 06510 (203) 432-5180. Its students are college graduates studying music performance and history, the arts and liturgy.

New York

The Juilliard School, 60 Lincoln Plaza, New York, NY 10023 (212) 799-5000. The ne plus ultra. Student ensembles are the big thing here—they tour the world. Good luck trying to get one for your wedding, but *you never know.*

The Manhattan School of Music, 120 Claremont Avenue, New York, NY 10027 (212) 749-2802. They're really good and really nice. Ask for Mark Laporta, the Placement Director.

Philadelphia

Academy of Vocal Arts, 1920 Spruce Street, Philadelphia, PA 19103 (215) 735-1685. It's free and extremely competitive. They're training for careers on the opera and concert stages of the world.

The Curtis Institute of Music, 1726 Locust Street, Philadelphia, PA 19103 (215) 893-5252. Pianists get free loan of a Steinway grand the whole time they're there, so they're *really* good.

San Francisco

San Francisco Conservatory of Music, 1201 Ortega Street, San Francisco, CA 94122 (415) 564-8086. Isaac Stern and Yehudi Menuhin studied here. Do you need to know more?

FOURTEEN CLASSICAL SELECTIONS

The following pieces are suitable for church organ, orchestra, or string ensemble, and are available on CDs and tapes:

1 "Wedding March" from *Lohengrin* (Wagner). "Here Comes the Bride"—use it for the Processional.
2 "Wedding March" from *A Midsummer Night's Dream* (Mendelssohn). Customary for Recessional.
3 "Jesu, Joy of Man's Desiring" (Bach)
4 "Ave Maria" (Schubert)
5 "The Lord's Prayer" (Malotte)
6 "The Voice That Breathed O'er Eden" (Haydn)
7 "Serenade" (Schubert)
8 "Trumpet Tune" (Purcell)
9 "Canon in D Minor" (Pachelbel)
10 "Water Music" (Handel)
11 "First Organ Sonata" (Mendelssohn)
12 "Hallelujah Chorus" from *The Messiah* (Handel)
13 "Ode to Joy" (Beethoven)
14 "Sheep May Safely Graze" (Bach)

LIMO LOGIC

os Angeles has greater distances; New York has more traffic; Boston is compact but bottlenecked. As geography and traffic conditions vary, so does the limousine picture around the country.

GENERAL GUIDELINES

• White and gold are more costly than black and gray.

• The white Seville stretch seating six passengers goes for somewhere around $200 for the three-hour minimum; such dream machines as the white Excalibur four-door sedan can be as much as $500 for three hours.
• You can often get a cloth runner, in white, red, or pink, but it costs extra.
• The limo companies do not like to drive the getaway car, and usually do not include it in the wedding package.

THE WEDDING PACKAGE
• Usually includes pickup at the bride's home, the trip to the ceremony, the trip to the reception—three to four hours in all.
• Should be arranged three months in advance of the wedding.

QUESTIONS TO ASK
• Would an hourly charge be more economical than the wedding package in our case?
• If we exceed the allotted time what are the incremental charges?
• Is the gratuity included in the fee? (Fifteen to 20 percent for the driver is usual.)
• Can we expect certain extras? (A VCR? Tapes? A CD player? A TV?)
• If the bar is stocked, will the liquor and/or champagne be of good quality?

Such reputable companies as Dav El Livery keep fleets in most cities; otherwise, trust word of mouth. Payment is made face to face as a rule; the company will not bill you, and the credit-card companies will no longer accept charges without verified signatures.

Some bridal couples have been known to be quite late to their own reception; this is through no fault of the driver, whose utmost discretion, not to mention double partition, is requested. As Ralph Duncan of Dav El puts it, "They don't want to get out of the vehicle. It's not just that they park somewhere. They move in."

espite the video revolution, brides continue to pose for traditional photographs. Why? Because they have been photographed ever since the invention of the camera. Because they want to linger over key moments later without having to push Pause. Because a portrait is a work of art with power of its own. And because the prints make nice gifts. These considerations lead to a choice: whether to hire a photographer from one of the big-name houses or search for a free-lancer. Whatever you decide, ask a friend to take snapshots, too. That way, you'll have some backup if for some reason the professional shots are duds.

HIRING A PHOTOGRAPHER FROM A BIG-NAME HOUSE. *Pluses:* A large urban studio has a stable of photographers available for weddings and can assemble a variety of albums (30–100 prints, typically) for you, your parents, your grandparents, your friends. The studio is likely to offer a wedding package; this may include a set number of prints for albums, framing, newspaper announcements, folders for your attendants, even wallet-sized mementoes to slip in with your thank-you notes. In other words, the big-name house has wedding photography down to a science.

Minuses: Many of the available studio photographers are just beginning their careers; others appear to have been catching brides on film since the days of Matthew Brady. In either case, the photographer at your wedding is paid only a small percentage of the fee the house is charging you, and as a result may not be as excited as you are to be at your wedding. Further, because studio business is based on keeping the film and charging a markup on every print sold, a lot of market research has gone into analyzing the shots that sell. They know what these shots are, as sure as they know it's the parents who actually buy the prints. As a result they send their wedding photographers out with very clear marching orders: *"Don't come back until you have these shots."* Does your photographer deserve a pushy reputation? It's probably be-

cause he can't return to headquarters until he has that formalized scene of you adjusting your veil in front of a mirror while your mother looks on. And a few more groupings of your parents' friends standing staring into the camera. And this humdinger: your father's boss waltzing with his wife.

HIRING A FREE-LANCER. *Pluses:* If you can locate a photographer who has experience shooting commercials or ads— shooting vignettes of human emotion, that is—your pictures may take on a very nice storytelling quality; ditto any photographer who, experience notwithstanding, is willing to work with you to customize the shots. (You may want to get a couple of candids beforehand of your everyday life at the office. Or, you may fancy some sort of departure after the ceremony—in La Jolla, for example, the adventurous bride pulls up to water's edge in her limo, to pose in her regalia in front of the sunset and all nature.) Some free-lancers charge a day rate and at the end of the job simply give you the film to develop (thus allowing you not only to create your own album but also to save some money). Such people are freer to look for the great moments occurring naturally and to find, rather than create, the logical portraits and groupings.

Minuses: A free-lancer is chancey, won't come with the imprimatur of a studio, and may not come at all.

To find a good photographer, follow the grapevine, phone the art director at a local ad agency for a reference, and/or get in touch with the Professional Photographers of America, 1090 Executive Way, Des Plaines, IL 60028.

rides from foreign lands want their adopted cities behind them. Longtime natives crave a backdrop of indigenous scenery. The environmentally aware wish to be as much a part of nature as they are of tradition. That's why the newest photographic trend makes the world your studio. (And the park in downtown Toronto your stomping ground, if you're one of the scores of brides who are photographed there on any given Saturday.) To ensure that such nuisances as heat, rain, and mosquitoes won't ruin their look, some brides prefer to schedule their outdoor portraits for a day after the wedding. The time is up to you. As for the space, however, Lydia May, Monty Zucker, David Ziser, Alvin Gee, Jack Curtis, Linda Smith, Donald Jack, Bruce Hudson, and Ron Stewart—award-winning professionals who know where the light is good on their turf—suggest these choice natural settings for breathtaking bridal portraits.

ATLANTA

The most beautiful shots are to be had in the rose gardens at Callenwolde, in DeKalb County. Another good bet is the plantation area at Stone Mountain—or even halfway up the mountain, especially at twilight, when Atlanta below and in the distance is ghostly and magical but not necessarily gone with the wind.

BOSTON

The Public Garden, by the swan boats, is a favorite spot. A good "360" can be taken from the bike path on Massachusetts Avenue. Stand on or near any of the bridges, with either Cambridge or downtown Boston behind you. For romance and charm, go out to Sudbury and pose in front of the Old Grist Mill.

CHICAGO

If you can get up to the ninety-fifth floor of the Hancock Building at night, you can see forever. Otherwise, the most popular spot is in Batavia: the Japanese garden in Fabian's Forest Preserve.

CINCINNATI

Stand on the Kentucky side of the Ohio River, with the Cincinnati skyline in the background and you'll know why-o to leave Ohio (at least for these pictures).

HOUSTON

For a wonderful shot showing the Houston skyline in the background, pose on the jogging path along Allen Parkway. Alternatively, try Tranquillity Park downtown.

LOS ANGELES

In Santa Monica, go down to the grassy park on Ocean Avenue at sunset and get the Pacific behind you. For an airy background with beautiful flowers, head for the Desconzo Gardens near Pasadena.

MIAMI

Get thee to a . . . monastery—the Spanish Monastery in North Miami Beach.

NEW YORK

Hit Central Park—the Sheep Meadow with the midtown skyline behind you anytime; or the Reservoir when the cherry trees are in blossom.

OMAHA

The stately elms of Mount Vernon Gardens set a nice tone from mid-April to the beginning of October, when the weather is quasi-dependable.

PROVIDENCE

Roger Williams Park = excellent!

SAN ANTONIO

Put history in your photos by standing on the River Walk. Or go to Breckenridge Park.

SAN FRANCISCO

In Tiburon, there's a spot behind the Community Congregational Church at

GOLDEN GATE BRIDGE   SAUSALITO

PHOTO © 1989 STEVEN YEAGER

JANELLE   MIKE

the top of Rock Hill Drive that yields a portrait of the bride with the Golden Gate Bridge over her right shoulder and Sausalito over her left.

SEATTLE

Far and away the most popular spot is Highland Park on Queen Anne Hill—you get Seattle (Space Needle and all) at eye level behind you.

WASHINGTON, D.C.

Definitely the view from the Lincoln Memorial, with the Reflecting Pool, the Washington Memorial, the Capitol dome as your backup.

MIND GAMES

Hurry Up and Wait

bout the groom's not seeing you on your wedding day until the actual ceremony: being confined to quarters derives from marriage by purchase, when the bride began to hide behind a veil not just to escape evil spirits but also to signal the world that no man could look upon her except the one who had paid for her (see Queen for a Day: Evolution and Semiotics of the Bride's Outfit, page 102). As it happens, though, brides in the United States didn't get into this custom until Victorian times, when prenuptial seclusion seems to have swept in with the pure-white wedding dress and all its connotations of innocence and chastity. After that, hiding out was like holding out—a nice girl did it, because she just didn't want to appear too eager. American brides, embracing the practice, killed time by getting dressed for the ceremony—still the recommended activity (allow two hours) if you're observing tradition.

Recently, however, a new trend has emerged. Certain discerning brides have begun to take the first hesitant steps out of seclusion. Instead of waiting all day to see their grooms at the ceremony, they're waiting only part of the day, and seeing them beforehand. And why? So they can have their photographs taken early. The usual photo opportunity, directly after the vows and before the reception, has become notorious among wedding guests as a potentially bathyscaphic trough in an otherwise vast sea of merrymaking. (Consider: If you, your groom, your closest relatives, and your dearest friends all disappear to have your pictures taken, just how much fun can the people you left behind have?)

The new strategy is to schedule a "private moment" before the ceremony when the bride in her finery welcomes the groom and he's the only one looking. This often happens in a garden, but a cleared and closed room is also dramatic. The approach has the advantage of being both highly efficient and also true to the spirit of the taboo—but in honesty even doing things this way leaves some preliminary down-time. So, in the quintessentially private (read: solitary) moment while you're waiting for your prince to come, don't just stand there—and don't sit, either, or you'll wrinkle your skirt. Try passing the minutes in one or several of these painless ways.

MAKE A MENTAL LIST. Everything you forgot to pack for the honeymoon is diverting food for thought.

EXAMINE YOUR MANICURE.

COUNT THE HOURS YOU'VE SLEPT IN THE PAST WEEK.

DANCE. These few seconds alone provide an excellent opportunity to discover if your dress moves the way they said it would during the fittings. (Of course, it's also an excellent opportunity to sprain your ankle.)

MAKE YOURSELF CRAZY. Go over the place cards in your mind just one more time.

WONDER WHAT'S KEEPING YOUR GROOM.

WONDER WHAT A NICE GIRL LIKE YOU IS DOING IN A PLACE LIKE THIS. You're standing here in a silly dress, about to get *married?* When you could have chosen instead to live by yourself, or with your cat, or cats, in a perfectly nice studio apartment, resolutely devoting yourself to your career.

THINK ABOUT THE PROFOUND SIGNIFICANCE OF MARRIAGE. You can't wear old T-shirts to bed anymore.

PLAN ON WINNING THE LOTTERY. With twenty million dollars to spend, your marriage could really get off to a good start!

All you have to do is dream up a meaningful number sequence and defy the odds. Your age, your groom's age, the day and month of this wedding might work. Or your birthday, your groom's birthday, the day and month of this wedding. Or—well, once you start working on this, you're apt to find *lots* of combinations to choose from.

IMAGINE YOURSELF AS THE KIND OF WIFE YOUR MOTHER WAS, AND YOUR GROOM AS THE KIND OF HUSBAND YOUR FATHER WAS. No, don't, Dr. Freud.

PRACTICE SMILING. A beauty contestant would put a film of Vaseline on her teeth, to make marathon grinning easier. But a beauty contestant won't be kissing your groom today. Unless you're a beauty contestant, that is.

PRAY. One out of two marriages fails—and one out of two doesn't.

PRAYING FOR RAIN

The Myth Behind the Ceremony

ou have arrived at the moment of truth—when saying a mere two little words, I will, will change your life. You might want to consider what you're doing. Historically speaking, this ceremony is all about your fertility. The symbols tell the story—you're surrounded by nuts and berries and seed-bearing plants (and probably can expect to be pregnant at any moment). It's been ever thus. *Viz:*

Almost every tribal community had some sort of Mother Earth, Father Sky myth, wherein the sky lay on top of the earth and watered it such that crops grew. Because crops were essential to the tribe's survival, the myth was extraordinarily powerful. What's more, each time it was acted out, the marrying (read: copulating) couple became extraordinarily powerful—so powerful, in fact, that the bride and groom were thought of as royalty and their ceremony as nothing less than a coronation. Members of the community, loyal subjects, provided group support—as did the ritual. Think of Adam and Eve as the primal wedding couple, and then think of what they went through to ensure that generations would beget generations and humankind would continue. Their effort and struggle were reflected in a ritual filled with sympathetic magic to help the bride not only lose her virginity but, more important, to give birth. Breaking something suggested breaking the hymen; the loosening of knots and laces suggested the removal of restrictive clothing during delivery. (Much of the ancient ceremony is easily observed today in the Jewish wedding ritual, the oldest of any in the world—and some of it is still seen in the Christian ceremony.)

With the rise of organized society, the observation of wedding ritual became a sign of status. Just as rulers had once acted as gods, now the nobility acted like rulers; before long, merchants started acting like nobility, celebrating *their* weddings with ritual, too. Completely ordinary people donned special clothing, often were crowned, and were treated like kings and queens. Enter the Church. To the early proselytizers, pretension was a starting point: by simply co-opting the old royal customs and adapting them for a developing Christian ceremony, they could work with the people. Things stayed the same as they became different. No one mentioned that Adam and Eve had been married only in the sight of God—getting married the religious way was here to stay, and getting to the church on time a universal concern. If today you choose to wed under nonreligious auspices—at city hall, say —the chances are still good that somewhere along the line you will invoke the All-Powerful. The long arm of centuries-old tradition has a fearful pull. Blessings on you.

ORDER OF . . .

The Processional

CHRISTIAN AND REFORM JEWISH

1 Ushers, according to height (shortest first)
2 Junior ushers (ages nine to fourteen)
3 Junior bridesmaids (ages nine to fourteen)
4 Bridesmaids, according to height (shortest first)
5 Maid or matron of honor
6 Flower girls (ages four to eight)
7 Ring bearer (age four to eight)
8 Bride, holding right arm of her father
The groom and best man wait at the altar with the clergyperson

ORTHODOX AND CONSERVATIVE JEWISH

1 Ushers
2 Bridesmaids
3 Rabbi and Cantor
4 Best man
5 Groom, accompanied by his mother and father
6 Maid of honor
7 Bride, walking between her mother and father

The Recessional

CHRISTIAN AND REFORM JEWISH

1 Bride and groom
2 Flower girl
3 Maid of honor and best man
4 Bridesmaids (behind bride) and ushers (behind groom)

ORTHODOX AND CONSERVATIVE JEWISH

1 Bride and groom
2 Bride's parents
3 Groom's parents
4 Maid of honor and best man
5 Flower girl
6 Rabbi
7 Cantor
8 Bridesmaids and ushers

WORDS TO LIVE BY

Some Views on Your Vows

 o you really want to make this commitment? You've already said yes, and the years ahead are unfolding before your eyes like a brightly colored travelogue of high points and sunny weather. But achieving a lifetime of bliss won't be easy. Certain ground rules must be laid down.

To begin, it's important to get clear what's being agreed upon. Obedience is largely out. Cherishing is in. The rest is negotiable. Whether you sing praises to the Lord or merely pledge to face the future side by side will depend on many factors. In fact, coming up with a ceremony both of you can live with is a process just about as intense as marriage itself—you may wish to go along with some or all of a service as written, but then again, you may also want to substitute some famous and/or obscure poetry, or offer a few words of your own.

Creativity is increasingly the norm, because it implies flexibility, which implies sharing and caring, which imply a successful modern marriage. Thus, a wispy slip of a bride may announce she means to spend the rest of her days as a soldier of love, while the cutest halfback of a groom may observe his winged adoration taking flight even as he speaks.

Any ceremony, standard or variation, runs the risk of being some combination of boring, ludicrous, off the subject, and too long. (The least chance of long-windedness occurs in a civil ceremony at city hall, a slam-bam situation if ever there was one, except that you usually have to wait around for your turn.) Some vows descend into a netherworld of reflection. You too may feel you absolutely have to drone on for a while before you can take the most important step of your life, or even leave for the reception hall.

On the other hand, maybe you'll remember the beauty in simplicity. If so, the ceremony at which you and your beloved exchange your vows could easily be totally moving, causing everyone to tear up, only to laugh at their own foolishness. If you can agree on the vows, you can make the commitment, and vice versa. In the end there's a beginning: two people are wed—no matter how they said it.

Some basic approaches to your very own marriage by consent:

PHOTOS/VERA

RELIGIOUS VOWS: A Roman Catholic bride and groom may be married at a wedding mass; a Protestant couple, at a celebration of marriage whose form varies among the denominations but usually includes a blessing of the ring. Jewish brides and grooms stand under the huppa for what are really two ceremonies melded into one, with several distinct sections: the ring ceremony, the voices of joy and gladness, the seven blessings, the finales. (*Note:* Traditionally, the Jewish bridal couple does not speak its vows, but many American rabbis and couples have added vows to be recited either just prior to or during the ring ceremony.)

SECULAR VOWS: You may be standing in a very interesting place that isn't a church or temple when you recite the great words of literature and/or the United Nations charter to set the tone for your marriage. If so, take some time before the wedding to consider how these words will sound—and if they can be heard —in the Rainbow Room, a mangrove swamp, your home. Then confer with the officiant about what you're planning. There are lots of books to get you started on choosing your selections (a nice one is *The Oxford Book of Marriage,* edited by Helge Rubinstein). After the reading from Queen Victoria's journal, the verse from Robert Frost, and the Chippewa Song, the actual vows can be as flowery or minimal as you like.

WRITING YOUR OWN VOWS: These can sound like the answers to the questions at a college interview if you're not careful. Favorite books, movies, and the moment that changed your perspective forever all are mentioned fondly, even with reverence. Those efforts that demonstrate a healthy respect for brevity are most effective. If you want the Wedding Vow Developmental Questionnaire write to Barbara Eklof, c/o Bob Adams Inc., 260 Center Street, Holbrooke, MA 02343. And block those metaphors—the ship of love on the highway of life.

A CHRISTIAN WEDDING CEREMONY

 early beloved, we are gathered here in the sight of God, and in the face of this company, to join together this man and woman in holy matrimony; which is commended of St. Paul to be honorable among all men; and therefore is not by any to be entered into unadvisedly or lightly; but reverently, discreetly, advisedly and soberly. Into this holy estate these two persons present come now to be joined. If any man can show any just cause why they may not lawfully be joined together, let him now speak or else hereafter forever hold his peace.

Wilt thou have this Woman to thy wedded wife, to live together after God's ordinance in the holy estate of matrimony? Wilt thou love her, comfort her, honor, and keep her in sickness and in health; and, forsaking all others, keep thee only unto her, so long as ye both shall live?

The groom answers: I will.

Wilt thou have this Man to thy wedded husband, to live together after God's ordinance in the holy estate of matrimony? Wilt thou love him, comfort him, honor, and keep him in sickness and in health; and, forsaking all others, keep thee only unto him, so long as ye both shall live?

The bride answers: I will.

Who giveth this Woman to be married to this man?

The bride's father or friend replies: "I do." The minister will then join the bride's right hand with the groom's right hand and the groom and bride, in turn, will repeat the following vows after the minister:

I [name] take thee [name] to my wedded wife/husband, to have and to hold from this day forward, for better for worse, for richer for poorer, in sickness and in health, to love and to cherish, till death do us part, according to God's holy ordinance; and thereto I plight thee my troth.

The bride and groom loose their hands, the groom places a ring on the bride's finger (and she may place a ring on his finger) and each in turn repeats after the minister:

With this Ring I thee wed, with my body I thee worship, and with all my worldly goods I thee endow: In the name of the Father, and of the Son, and of the Holy Ghost. Amen.

The Lord's Prayer and other prayers may be said. Then the minister joins the bride's and groom's right hands and says:

Those whom God hath joined together, let no man put asunder.

THE HEBREW SEVEN BLESSINGS

 lessed are you, Holy One of the Earth, who creates the fruit of the vine.

Blessed are you, Holy One of the Universe. You created all things for your glory.

Blessed are you, Holy One of the World.

Through you mankind lives.

Blessed are you, Holy One of the World. You made man and woman in your image, after your likeness, that they might perpetuate life. . . .

Blessed are you, Holy One of all Nature, who makes Zion rejoice with her children. . . .

Blessed are you, Holy One of the Cosmos, who makes the bridegroom and bride to rejoice.

Blessed are you, Holy One of All, who created joy and gladness, bride and bridegroom, mirth and song, pleasure and delight, love, fellowship, peace and friendship. . . .

BREAKING THE GLASS

t the end of the Jewish wedding ceremony, the groom crushes a glass under his heel. What does this symbolize? Eight interpretations:
- The breaking of the bride's hymen
- The fragility of human relationships
- The noisy chasing away of demons
- The destruction of the Temple
- The idea that even in the midst of rejoicing there should be trembling
- The ancient way a congregation kept its thirsty rabbis in line at a wedding—by smashing their good goblets right in front of them
- A goodbye to the past
- The end of the ceremony

Mazel tov!

CREATING A JEWISH-CHRISTIAN CEREMONY

ccording to estimates, some 125,000 Jewish-Christian couples marry annually in the United States. Add to their numbers all those brides and grooms who are already "half-and-half"—the children of the Jewish-Gentile marriages of the 1960s—and it's clear many, many interfaith marriages are taking place. What are the ceremonies like? Fractious? Harmonious?

Yes.

If you're planning an interfaith ceremony, the operative word is planning. Lee Gruzen, interfaith expert and author of *Raising Your Jewish-Christian Child*, advises a course of action that goes something like this:

STEP ONE: Talk to other Jewish-Christian couples. Someone who's just been through this experience is your best source—which is to say your clergyperson isn't. The minister, the priest, the rabbi will give you information and may even be sympathetic, but the clergy's interests are fundamentally different from yours. There's tradition, and then there's the new way you're trying to modify it. It's a problem.

STEP TWO: Find the clergy who will agree to perform the ceremony. This is far more difficult than you may expect—with the result that you may be reduced to scouring the society page of the newspaper for accounts of weddings performed by both a rabbi and minister. (When you come upon these people, call them.) Some priests and ministers won't enter a synagogue. And as if that weren't harsh enough—well, an eager rabbi is hard to find (unless he's one of the so-called "mercenaries," who, for a hefty fee, will perform a Jewish-style wedding for a Jew and non-Jew). As a rule, Orthodox and Conservative rabbis never officiate at a mixed marriage, while some Reform and Reconstructionist rabbis do, but most don't. (The results of a 1978 survey of 1,268 rabbis: only a handful, 157, said they had officiated at an intermarriage.) The permutations and gradations of rabbi-willingness are therefore manifold—most will not co-officiate (but a few will, simply because they wish to see the Jewish faith represented); some will consider presiding only if you pledge to raise the children as Jews; some will require several meetings with the couple; and so on. It's not a personal rejection, it's a matter of Jewish law, but suffice it to say the rabbi who saw you through your bar mitzvah cannot be counted upon to marry you. Many couples ultimately consult Rabbi Irwin Fishbein, 128 East Dudley Avenue, Westfield, NJ 07090 (908) 233-2288; for $15, he will provide a list of 200 rabbis nationwide who will participate, at least to some degree, in interfaith ceremonies. Other couples decide to waive the clergy in favor of a secular authority who will perform a ceremony with religious symbols and content.

STEP THREE: Chances are you've agreed to be married on neutral territory, rather than in a house of worship. If God is in all things, and everywhere, it's nice to select a site—the windswept cliff, the lush garden—where His presence is obvious. Still, even a nondescript situation can work for you if you make it feel like the sanctuary it has become. Bring in a huppa, some musicians, flowers, gentler lighting.

STEP FOUR: Create the ceremony. The key, say many couples who've been through it, is to establish an atmosphere that's reverent but not superreligious. Typically, both faiths are acknowledged (Minister: "May you learn to love and respect his faith as you love and respect your own"; Rabbi: "May you learn to love and respect her faith as you love and respect your own"). Jesus will probably not be mentioned by name. The *haray aht* may be omitted or changed. Many clergy discuss the symbol of the candle. Blessings are from the Old Testament, usually culminating in "May his face shine upon you and give you peace." And the glass is broken.

STEP FIVE: Arrange the reception. The common mistake is going overboard—you don't have to eat every delicacy and knish known to both religions any more than you have to dance the polka and the hora both at the same time. (Although it's an idea.)

STEP SIX: Deal with the difficult relative. Interfaith couples say there's almost always at least one. An aunt who refuses to attend the ceremony; the father who makes an awkward toast redolent with New Testament references; the grandmother who faints. Author Gruzen suggests getting to these people before the ceremony, both to solicit their ideas for touches to include in the ceremony and to assign them a "buddy" to ease the way. Gruzen also believes interfaith couples should test out a seder, or have a Christmas and Hanukkah together, before they marry. Experiencing each other's basic traditions is good research for the wedding. And creating harmony among the in-laws can't begin a moment too soon.

WHEN THE LOVEBIRDS ARE PIGEONS

 t some weddings, birds are let loose only moments after the bride and groom are pronounced man and wife. This is not good! According to a spokesperson for the Dawn Animal Agency in New York, turning two birds loose in a crowd of strangers is frightening to the birds, especially if the people start to swat at them. It's far better to plan a controlled, choreographed situation that's fair to bird and bride: the bird should be safe; the bride

should get the effect she wants. At Dawn, and its affiliates in Florida and California, this can mean the birds become part of a medieval pageant starring the bride but also featuring white horses and deer; or it can mean accompanying a horse-drawn carriage; or—but never mind. Dawn is state-of-the-art when it comes to handling animals for all sorts of theater, including (and they're not always so easily distinguishable) circuses and weddings. Use their guidelines if you feel your wedding is for the birds:

• Aim to create good feelings, not a nuisance.
• Make sure a trainer comes with the birds.
• Because doves are poor fliers with soft wings, use them indoors only. (Releasing them outdoors will strand them, and eventually they'll starve.)
• If you wish to release birds outdoors—say, as you exit the church—use white homing pigeons.
• Make sure the pigeons have enough time to make it home in the daylight hours. (Dawn's pigeons return to their home in upstate New York; from Manhattan they need a tail wind and a few hours.) Never release pigeons outdoors in the late afternoon or evening.
• Find out what the birds are doing when they're not working a wedding. Homing pigeons should not be caged, because their wings can be damaged if they're not allowed to fly every day.

Dawn Animal Agency, New York (212) 575-9396; Cougar Hill, Los Angeles (805) 944-3549; Janice Aria, Orlando, Florida (813) 422-4080; fees dependent on the wedding's location, time, breadth of vision.

he bride is so beautiful that she lives forever in memory. Also on videotape, where her image actually smiles, kisses, dances, and even *talks*. If *The Jazz Singer* brought about a revolution in Hollywood, and "An American Family" changed TV forever, it is the video that has blown away the contemporary wedding. America's funniest brides are the subject of video parties that ushers hold when they return to their homes across the country; total strangers become hooked on two hours of Rochelle in her gown. Similarly, the newlyweds play the tape over and over, potential aphrodisiac for some, comforting background for all—meals are eaten, bills are paid, the apartment is vacuumed while Uncle Herman once again makes a pass at the vocalist. Relatives who receive complimentary copies of the videotape just can't believe how long the thing is. Well, no one can.

SHOULD YOU HIRE A VIDEOGRAPHER? Yes. Otherwise you'll go through the next fifty years without being able to pop the tape into the VCR whenever you want to feel young and thin. And Mommy being a bride is almost as fascinating to your unborn children as "Sesame Street."

HOW DO YOU HIRE A VIDEOGRAPHER? Call the Society of Professional Videographers, in Huntsville, Alabama (205) 534-3600, and get a list of referrals in your area. What the Society wants you to know: wedding videography is still so new that substandard standards are by no means a thing of the past among amateurs. Horror stories have to do with tapes being lost, or grainy, or dark, or spliced so that some other bridal couple suddenly appears on your tape. Photographers belong to a profession that has spent years establishing itself; videographers don't. Therefore, cautions the Society, ask to view more than one display tape even if you have glowing references, because if a videographer is showing only one tape, chances are it's his best, not the one where he messed up the audio. And make sure he visits the reception site before the wedding.

SHOULD THE VIDEOGRAPHERS USE ONE CAMERA OR TWO? The buzz word in wedding videography is "unobtrusive." If the "Eyewitness News" crew is obviously obtrusive, so also are two cameras likely to be more obtrusive than one. Still, if you want reaction shots you're probably going to have to have them. Set some ground rules so that no one steps on your grandmother's bunion just as you say "I will." Then relax.

SHOULD THE MUSIC BE DUBBED OR SHOULD YOU COUNT ON THE VIDEO TO PICK UP WHATEVER THE DJ IS PLAYING? Up to you. Some couples feel they don't want to pay for canned music that may seem dated later on; for them, the basic no-frills, bargain-basement $200 video is preferable. Others say good music helps the pacing of the video; these couples may elect the "music over."

SHOULD THE VIDEO BE A STRAIGHT RECORDING OF YOUR WEDDING DAY OR...SOMETHING MORE? There are certain basic shots you probably don't want to overlook. They are, in sequence: the procession, the vows, the bridal kiss, the first dance, the cake, the leavetaking. Your involvement in these images (which, in ideal circumstances, will unfold unobtrusively in a non-stage-managed, completely natural photojournalistic fashion) makes you the newest version of every bride who's gone before you; it places you in the daisy chain of the generations, the movie of life, the sisterhood of man. Now you're one of the crowd. That being said, a little self-importance could be sweet; at a cost of approximately $1,000, some videographers include such extras as titles, baby photos, shots of your wedding invitation, a dream sequence, a flashback ending. If your videographer wants to take a documentary approach, or an art piece featuring aerial shots of you walking on the beach in your wedding dress, the results could very well be intriguing. Or truly, truly embarrassing.

he Man on the Street interview, long a favorite of print and TV reporters, is now embraced by wedding videographers. You're exiting the ceremony, just discovering everything you have in common with the copywriter the bride shared an office with two ad agencies ago. Suddenly, you're bathed in a sepulchral light and there's a microphone in your face. You're on! Some possibilities the next time you're asked to tell us what you care to about the bridal couple:

• Sing—anything, with wide open arms and a big kiss at the end.
• Reminisce about a field trip you and the groom took in fourth grade.
• Deliver a little homily. "Love is blind; marriage is the eye opener" is a favorite.
• Begin an off-color joke, such as the one about Little Red Riding Hood and the wolf.

Shrink Think 3

What are your brother and sister going through as you plan for your wedding day? Just when you'd sort of forgotten them, psychotherapist Karen Faircloth hasn't. She can tell you about their emotions on and around your big day.

Dear Therapist Karen:
My brother and sister are acting impossible. My sister—younger by two years—just cut her hair so short she's going to look like a freak at the wedding. And my brother—older—has decided to stop smoking and can't do anything but talk about how many minutes, hours, days it's been since he's had a cigarette. I realize everyone wants attention, but give me a break! What should I do?

Sibling Rival

Dear Sibling Rival:
I like your signature: you know exactly what is going on—your siblings are competitive with you and can't help acting it out. Try to remember what you've already learned in the past about living with them; you

already know a lot. And don't worry: the day of the wedding *everyone* will have eyes and ears only for you, the bride. You'll win then.

Congratulations!
Karen

I DO?

Do you know what you're saying? Maybe, but some bridal couples become easily confused when it's time to seal the marriage contract. To avoid taking a pledge or reciting some words you didn't quite intend, test yourself by matching each numbered phrase with the correct lettered source. Answers at the bottom.

1 "Let me not to the marriage of true minds admit impediments."

2 "With this ring I thee wed, with my body I thee worship, and with all my worldly goods I thee endow."

3 "By this ring you are consecrated to me in accordance with the traditions of Moses and Israel."

4 "For all my life I offer myself to you."

5 "Love one another, but make not a bond of love: Let it rather be a moving sea between the shores of your souls."

6 "Until the day break, and the shadows flee away, I will get me to the mountain of myrrh, and to the hill of frankincense."

7 "Congress shall make no law respecting an establishment of religion, or prohibiting the free exercise thereof; or abridging the freedom of speech, or of the press; or the right of the people peaceably to assemble, and to petition the government for a redress of grievances."

8 "Fellow-citizens, we cannot escape history."

(a) Kahlil Gibran, *The Prophet*
(b) *The Book of Common Prayer*
(c) Jewish Ring Ceremony
(d) W. S. Shakespeare, Sonnet CXVI

(e) *Song of Solomon*
(f) You wrote it yourself
(g) Amendment 1, U.S. Constitution
(h) Abraham Lincoln's annual message to Congress, 1862

Answers: 1.d; 2.b; 3.c; 4.f; 5.a; 6.e; 7.g; 8.h

• It wasn't until the Council of Trent in 1563 that the Roman Catholic Church declared any marriage not performed by a priest null and void.

• In seventeenth-century Virginia, colonists could simply nail a notice to the church door announcing they were married.

• Wedding ceremonies have been performed in an aquarium at Sea World in Orlando, Florida, and on the Revolution Roller Coaster in Valencia, California.

• The first publicized nude wedding took place at the Garden of Eden at the 1934 World's Fair in Chicago.

• Frank Sinatra's garden in Palm Springs, California, was the site of the November 1990 wedding of model Cheryl Tiegs to actor Tony Peck (son of Gregory).

• At Mick Jagger's second wedding, to Jerry Hall (in 1990, in Bali, after twelve years and two children together), the bride and groom both signed a statement affirming their conversion to Hinduism.

• New York City performs more than 37,000 marriage ceremonies a year, at the City Clerk's office in Manhattan's Municipal Building.

• The Jewish wedding ceremony is the oldest still surviving—its origins, modified in the eleventh century, date back to tribal life some three thousand years ago.

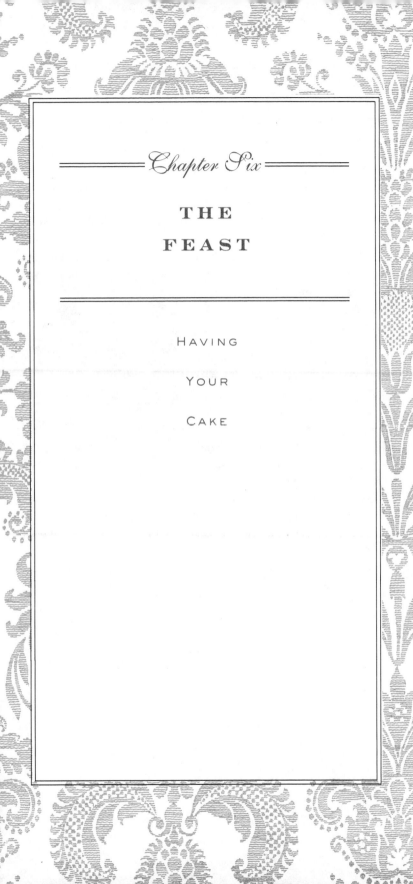

Chapter Six

THE
FEAST

HAVING

YOUR

CAKE

he tradition of feasting, music, and dance following the moment the bride is given in marriage resounds throughout history; who cleans up is someone else's problem. The bride and groom are at the center of the party, but the reception is really for everyone the couple has brought together. The bridal pair make an entrance, perhaps waving regally from a balcony several feet above the crowd (ask your bridal consultant), and commence the revelry, but they could never do the conga line by themselves. If they are the king and queen, the guests are their subjects, and the festivities celebrate the fact of the whole kingdom's ability to continue. In Jewish tradition, the bride and groom were entertained with jokes, reminiscences, magic tricks, poems, juggling routines, songs, and dances—and in any culture it's time to be happy. Thank you, bride, for keeping us going. And nice work, groom, getting her into this. Deck the halls with a lot of symbols of your fertility. Strike up the band. Here's to life! Maybe we'll even get some rain to water the crops.

180

PHOTO COURTESY DESIGNER WEDDINGS AND LYDIA MAY STUDIOS, CAMBRIDGE, MASSACHUSETTS

THE WEDDING AS VACATION

A City-by-City Guide to Diversions

onsider two trends: (a) families are scattered all over the country; (b) travelers are taking shorter, more frequent, vacations. Now consider the point at which the trends intersect: at a wedding.

All over the country, couples are rising to the challenge. As they approach their nuptials, brides and grooms are learning how to become not just husbands and wives, but entertainment directors and tour guides. Their far-flung guests arrive at an urban destination, a country resort, a corporate retreat. The tennis tournament is about to start (the best man has your seed number); the excursion to the glass factory is already under way; the triathlon is later. If love is in the air, so is civic pride: a brochure written and illustrated by the bride was included with the invitations, and a map and itinerary are in the welcome basket along with the cookies and matches (Alison and Bob's Wedding, June 18, 1992) and splits of champagne.

So, good morning, campers! You won't be sorry you've come. There's sure to be a wild scene at the bed and breakfast tonight, and meanwhile, don't forget Bridesmaids and Ushers' Tag Team Football on the beach. Please consult your personal schedule for the activities you checked off. And have fun. We're here to serve you. The shopping trip to the mall is leaving *now*.

You can't see everything. And with that hangover, you may not want to see anything. But how about something? Host brides and grooms advise out-of-town guests to squeeze in the following memorable activities—as long as they're back in time for the ceremony:

ATLANTA. Tell an usher he looks like General Robert E. Lee, whose likeness is carved into the side of Stone Mountain. Take the tram to the top to check it out. Climb back down. For the rest of the wedding, affectionately refer to the usher as "Bobby Lee."

BALTIMORE. Hit the Lexington Market—it's like going to a fair and there are open-air food stalls. Treat yourself to the raw bar, the bread, the cotton candy, the french fries, the beer. Great place to recover from the night before.

BOSTON. Take the T to Cambridge and head straight for the Cafe Pamplona (across the street from Adams House). It's been there ever since the heyday of coffeehouses and beatniks. Below ground, very small and cramped, doesn't serve alcohol (or much food, for that matter)—but you can smoke cigarettes, discuss your philosophy of life, gossip. And oh, that espresso!

CHICAGO. Mostly, it's so cold in Chicago they all stay indoors, but should you want to keep going after the welcoming cocktail party, try the deep-dish pizza at Gino's East on Superior. And the best jazz is at the Get Me High Lounge in Bucktown.

DETROIT. On a clear night, find "Ren Cen," which is what they call the Renaissance Center. Go up to the restaurant on top of the Westin Hotel (it rotates, for a panoramic view) with someone you just met. Twirl around. Alternatively, take the Tunnel Bus to Windsor, Ontario. Go to either Jason's or Cheetah's for the strip show and the nude table dancing.

LAS VEGAS. Leave the neon behind and head for the Red Rock Mountains. Get out and hike. Be with the desert. Ponder marriage as the union of souls. Get back in the car. Thank the gods and spirits for four-wheel drive.

LOS ANGELES. Ditch the rental Toyota in favor of the bride's brother's convertible VW and run out to the Huntington Museum (in San Marino) to see Gainsborough's "Blue Boy" and Lawrence's "Pinkie." On the way back to the parking lot, walk through the cactus garden.

MEMPHIS. Remember Elvis for either one and a half hours or a full three and a half hours: during your layover at the Memphis hub, simply bolt the airport and jump in a cab for the ten-minute ride to Graceland. Tickets for the shorter tour are $7.95; the longer one (including the house, the gravesite, a movie, his tour bus, and his plane) are $15.95.

NEW YORK. Ride the subway. Take the F train to Fourteenth Street. Stand at the front window of the very first car; watch the scene as you enter and leave stations. Then walk north to Twenty-first Street between Fifth Avenue and the Avenue of the Americas and shoot some pool at Chelsea Billiards.

PHILADELPHIA. This isn't just a city of connubial bliss, it's the City of Brotherly Love. Find Independence Hall. There's the Liberty Bell, cracked but intact. Pause to make the analogy to marriage. Then go get a cheese steak.

PITTSBURGH. Drive around Squirrel Hill, then down by all

three of the rivers, then back up a hill again. This is great! Like a roller coaster! Swing by Carnegie-Mellon. Ride up and down Forbes Avenue. Check out the new, unpolluted air. It almost makes you lightheaded. What a pretty city!

SAN FRANCISCO. Walk across the Golden Gate Bridge at sunset. There's a parking lot at the Presidio where you can leave the car, and there are bathrooms on the other side. On a rare day you can see the Farillon Islands, where sea lions live.

WASHINGTON, D.C. Beat the crowds—take a midnight tour of the monuments, when they're gloriously floodlit. The Jefferson Memorial, on the shimmering waters of the Tidal Basin, is the most romantic. There's never a fee. Just walk right in.

THE CUTTING EDGE

Decorating with Flowers

he flowers at your wedding can easily cost as much as your parents spent on rent the first year they were married, but what the hey—they signify your fruitfulness. Just look at these babies! They're everywhere—in centerpieces, swags, baskets; on arches, the staircases, the mantel. Brides choose exquisite, fragrant flowers with all the care they may ultimately lavish on their beautiful, sweet-smelling children. Champagne roses are popular because they open so nicely; lilacs are favored as well. To scent the air, fill a fountain with gardenias or go wild with tuberoses. To please the eye, mass orchids, lilies, freesias, snapdragons, and foxglove. Your floral look can take off from your color scheme, your personality, or your budget, and range from Victorian wildflowers to modern hothouse. Follow the seasons— use new blossoms in spring and summer, things from the field and harvest in autumn, silvery branches in winter. Schedule an inter-

view with the florist to see what's possible. Chrysanthemums and mums need not apply.

Some leading flower shops:

BOSTON

THE DUTCH FLOWER GARDEN, 12 Eliot Street, Cambridge, MA 02138 (800) 292-5459

CHICAGO

JASON RICHARDS, 363 West Chicago Avenue, Chicago, IL 60610 (312) 664-0605

DALLAS

MILLE FLEURS, 5100 Beltline Road, Suite 860, Dallas, TX 75240 (214) 960-1021

LOS ANGELES

FLORAL CREATIONS, 3351 La Cienega Place, Los Angeles, CA 90016 (800) 421-1790

NEW YORK

SURROUNDINGS, 224 W. 79th Street, New York, NY 10024 (212) 580-8982

WESTPORT, CONNECTICUT

THE FLOWER BASKET, 995 Post Road E., Westport, CT 06880 (203) 222-0206

PHOTO COURTESY SPITZ AND PECK FLORISTS, NEW YORK

Floralwise, the most cost-effective time to be married is as far away on the calendar as possible from a major holiday, and at a time of year when the flower you prize is abundant. For example, if you like tulips, marry in the spring when they're priced around four dollars a bunch—and don't even think about Christmastime, when they may be as high as twelve dollars a bunch.

BECAUSE FLOWER PRICES ARE EXORBITANT, AND BECAUSE THEY FLUCTUATE

EVERY GUEST IS A SUBPLOT

Ten Principles of the Receiving Line

 our invitations had a whopping 92 percent rate of constructive return. Everyone's here. Some people from the past you'd rather forget. Some people from the past you actually have. Exactly how mystified you are about several individuals' identity should never be revealed—just relax and maybe you'll remember the names you and your mother wrote out when you struggled with the place cards. Your receiving line may be at the church immediately following the ceremony—or maybe you're at the reception site and Uncle Herman is already complaining there are just too many people for the size of the room—but in either case, relax!

1 RELAXATION. You see, is the first principle of the receiving line. Here are the other nine:

2 COMFORTABLE SHOES. Brides are expected to stand for hours without looking as though their feet are killing them. Therefore, it's probably wise to accessorize your dream dress with something other than stiletto heels or the new, lower, white satin walking shoe with the vamp from hell.

3 WATER. Brides never gag in the receiving line if they can help it. And they can, if they keep themselves hydrated. Many brides like to have a glass of water handy for sipping. (Others just use champagne, as per Principle 10.)

4 SMILING. A trip to the dentist is the last stop before marriage for many couples—not just because of the pictures that will follow them through the years, but also because of the face-to-face contact with all these people. The big grin is the hallmark of a joyful couple. That it may cause soreness in the cheek muscles is just another reason to go on a honeymoon and get massaged all over.

5 FRIENDLINESS. A thinking bride could stand in for Miss Congeniality. (And *she* never had to deal all at once with your stepparents, neither of whom is speaking to your husband's parents; and your boss, who fired your maid of honor the day

before the wedding; and your husband's ex-girlfriend, who's also a dear family friend.) The bride on the receiving line acknowledges everyone individually. She avoids any mention of the horror with which her guest's acceptance, at $130 a head, was greeted by her mother. She makes him believe she just sort of couldn't have gotten married unless he'd been here. And he is! And she'd like to present him to . . .

6 TRUSTWORTHY EARRINGS. Even those brides who are expert at being kissed and hugged are careful their jewelry is secure. The diamond clip that fits snugly on your lobe is preferable to the one that accidentally drops into Grandfather's shirt front and can't be found, leaving you sick with loss until much, much later when the old gentleman finally retires for the evening.

7 MINIMALISM. Rather than creating a queue that's out the door and onto the sidewalk, somewhat resembling a crowd waiting to get into a hit movie, some brides elect to shorten the receiving line. The long-form sequence—mother of the bride, father of the bride (optional), mother of the groom, father of the groom, bride, groom, maid of honor, bridesmaids, ushers and best man—is modified: the fathers and attendants circulate among the guests while the bride, the groom, and their mothers do the formal welcoming. Another application of the minimalist principle lies in the greeting; whoever stands in the receiving line keeps the hellos warm but truly simple. Minimalism should never be mingy, however. On the contrary, it should connote concentration on the essence of the thing, graceful execution being both stimulus and relief. Put simply, less is more.

8 FLOW. The bottlenecked receiving line tends to irritate people in the back, who may grow paranoid and believe they're always on the tail end of everything. Brides therefore master certain eye movements and suggestive body language hinting at not only their unsurpassed pleasure in this particular moment but also the drinks, canapés, and diverting company farther on. They do not, repeat, *do not*, seize this opportunity to tie up the loose ends of frazzled relationships and/or pass out their business cards.

9 ETIQUETTE. Brides always get it right. This is because they've either been taught formal manners in their family, or have learned them from consultants, or have conscientiously read up and practiced beforehand. (Answer: the last one.) Information is readily available on how to make a correct introduction without being stiff—check Emily Post, Miss Manners, others. Meanwhile, remember at all times that etiquette is the bride's friend. Brides

use etiquctte as the ticket that can take them over any terrain, no matter how awkward.

10 A PARTY ATMOSPHERE. It's possible to have fun at your own wedding, even in the reception line. Naturally outgoing brides adore falling upon their wayward cousins and their father's paper supplier—and more reserved types revel in having gotten through the ceremony and this far without fainting (if they didn't). Music, manageable food, a nongauntlet configuration add festive touches to the receiving line, the gateway to the reception.

KISS LIST

The fifty people most likely to kiss you on your wedding day:

1 Your mother

2 Your father

3 Your brother

4 Your sister

5 Your half brother

6 Your half sister

7 Your stepbrother

8 Your stepsister

9 Your aunt

10 Uncle Herman

11 Your boss

12 Your old pediatrician

13 The minister

14 Gran

15 Gramps

16 Nana

17 Zayde

18 Jeff, from your husband's sleepaway camp

19 Jeff, from the Dukakis campaign

20–22 The brunch bunch

23 Your uncle's date, whose daughter went to Princeton with your sister

24 Your sister's boyfriend, who once went out with your uncle's date's daughter

25 A really important potential client of your father's

26 The legend in his own time, whom everyone wants to be photographed with

27 Your college roommate

28 Her fiancé

29 Your bridal consultant

30–33 Your neighbors in the one-bedroom apartment (they made their own partitions) down the hall from the thing you kept renting until you were officially married

34 Your assistant who wants your job one day

35 Your assistant who wants it right now

36 The guy whom Louise, your bridesmaid, just had to bring because she met him last weekend on her ski trip and it's been unreal ever since

37 Amy, your bridesmaid who was recently jilted and can barely stop crying, even for the pictures

38 Theresa, from Legal

39 The ring bearer, who had a tantrum just as the processional started

40–44 All four of your husband's grandparents, including his mother's mother, who can really boogie

45 Jean-Jacques, from the language immersion

46 The most notorious drunk in the entire history of the Cornell chapter of Theta Delta, which is saying something

47 The nice quiet usher

48–49 Your parents' next-door neighbors

50 Your husband

SEATING

For a buffet, or a seated luncheon or dinner, make out a seating plan and place cards. The standard configuration when no one has been divorced, widowed, or remarried:

Bride and Groom's Table

• Bride and groom together
• Maid of honor on groom's left
• Best man on bride's right
• Their spouses or companions
• Senior bridesmaids and their escorts
• Possibly the ushers (and their spouses or companions), but you may wish to scatter them among the other tables

Parents' Table

- Mother of the bride in the center
- Father of the groom on her right
- Father of the bride on her left
- Mother of the groom on his right
- Grandparents, godparents, officiant—alternating according to gender

Other Attendants

- May sit at the bridal table or at a table of their own, with their spouses or companions, or scattered about
- Keep child attendants with their parents

THE BEAT GOES ON: DANCE MUSIC

ome bridal couples could care less about dancing; all through the reception they simply keep the harp music going (see Going to School, page 149). Most newlyweds prefer to get down, however, and may even have bused in the entire Hank Lane group (will thirty pieces be enough?) at $300 to $350 a head. The bride hitches her train into a bustle, or detaches it altogether; the groom removes his jacket. The music they dance to at the party part of their wedding is so loud it may cause the floor to ripple frighteningly, reminding everyone that architectural disasters do happen . . . but never mind.

A wedding of 150 guests needs a three- or four-piece band; six or seven pieces are required for more guests. Prices differ around the country, but $2,000 for an evening wedding is not atypical. Every band in the land will send you a video, or—on the theory that each time they play they audition—invite you to the wedding of strangers. Lucky that this is one area where parents tend not to involve themselves in a power struggle. It's your opportunity to make a statement. Try to refrain from the backlash "I don't want Madonna at my wedding," which is all that band directors are hearing these days. Remember that, as a bride, you are the princess of peace and above politics. The various possibilities for dance music generally can be discovered within one of the following basic categories.

SOCIETY BANDS. Meyer Davis, Peter Duchin, Bill Harrington, Lester Lanin all play anywhere in the country—all you have to do is call their offices in New York one year in advance

PHOTO COURTESY EMERY AND MEYER DAVIS ORCHESTRA

and start negotiating. Say you're in Chicago and must have the Meyer Davis Orchestra. For $10,000 he'll take care of everything, including transportation for everyone he brings. See? It's easy. (Then again, in Chicago, you might want to substitute the Frank York Orchestra.) Society bands play a lot of Cole Porter and Glenn Miller, but they pride themselves on their rock and roll and Motown too, and they will definitely listen to your suggestions, even if your ideas aren't the same as the Du Ponts' about weddings. Lester Lanin (his motto: *optimum in musica*) is the one who gives out the beanies. He played at the receptions of Prince Charles and Princess Diana and Billy Joel and Christie Brinkley. No one knows how old he is.

VOLUME BANDS. Under one name and one sound, there are several groups; maybe they'll play as many as twelve weddings in one weekend. They are like society bands but cheaper. Examples are the Cabot Scott band in New York, the famed Hank Lane on Long Island, Billy Haynes and the Fabulous Charmers in Los Angeles.

CONCERT GROUPS. You found them at the local conservatory (see Eleven Top Music Schools, page 151) or hired your sister's group, modeled after 10,000 Maniacs. The concert group tends to be in-depth good at only one kind of music—notably jazz or rock and roll—but often they'll try anything.

ETHNIC BANDS. They can take over, be too loud for the old people to enjoy—but when they're good, it's worth it. There's nothing like reggae on the back lawn, or the badchan and klezmer at a swank hotel. The caterer knows where they are.

DJS. Look under Disc Jockeys or Entertainment in the Yellow Pages. This way, you can have swing, contemporary, jazz, rock, New Age, Yanni Procession, the Talking Heads, Kid Creole and the Coconuts, Monteverdi, anything.

THE AMERICAN FEDERATION OF MUSICIANS

hen the band starts talking about union rules, this is the union they mean. There are different locals, with different pay scales. In most parts of the country, the basic engagement is for three hours (in New York, it's four); typically, the musicians play twenty minutes and take a ten-minute break (in New York, they play fifty-five minutes and take a five-minute break). When you sign a contract with musicians, be specific about times. Otherwise, you may find yourself surprised by the silences and/or paying considerable overtime.

DANCE CARD

n the child's song, the mouse takes the cheese and the groom takes a wife, and it's all worked out who dances with whom, and when. It's the same way at a wedding. According to protocol, this is the order of dances:

　　1. The bride and groom begin the first dance together, the only couple on the dance floor.

2. The father of the bride cuts in; the groom dances with the mother of the bride.

3. The father and mother of the groom join the dancers. (If they're not married to each other anymore, the two of them can dance with each other anyway or come on the floor with their new spouses. Or other children. Or *someone*—don't let them sit it out; make arrangements.)

4. The attendants join the dancers.

5. The guests join the dancers.

HOW TO DO THE HORA

he hora is the Israeli national dance, performed at all sorts of celebrations, including Jewish weddings. It can be danced to various tunes, so long as the 2/4 time signature is observed, but most people associate it with "Hava Nagila." The hora's roots are in the most ancient forms of dance, which stressed tribal unity. Therefore, it is a dance done without partners. Dancers stand in a circle with their hands on the nearest shoulders of both their neighbors. The dance may be performed moving to the left or to the right. (The directions below are for movement to the right. Simply reverse everything to move to the left.) At a large wedding, the group may be divided into two circles, one inside the other, one going to the right, one going to the left. Variations abound; playfulness is the norm. Perhaps all the women will circle the bride, and all the men circle the groom, with each dancer entering the middle to take a turn with the bridal king or queen. Then, at the peak of the hilarity, the bride and groom are raised above their guests in chairs. They're twirled around each other, holding only the ends of a shared handkerchief. It's dizzying up there—to the point

KARA LEVERTE

that the newlyweds may have had to become inebriated before allowing themselves to be elevated, and many brides and grooms become airsick—but what can you do? Nausea in this context is a mitzvah.

To brush up on the hora at home:

1. Step to the side with your right foot.

2. Step behind your right foot with your left foot.

3. Step to the side again with your right foot.

4. Hop on your right foot. (Some people like to swing their left leg across their right leg as they hop on the right foot, but this is optional.)

5. Step to the side again with your left foot.

6. Hop on the left foot. (Again, you may wish to swing your right leg across your left leg while hopping on your left leg.)

7. Repeat steps 1–6.

THE TOASTS

rink enough champagne and anyone is eloquent, or at least capable of running off at the mouth. Giving a toast at the reception is not properly an opportunity for tastelessness, however. (Tastelessness is traditionally confined to the rehearsal dinner, where among only the closest family members and the wedding party, references to the groom's famous "hotter than the African sun, cooler than the Atlantic Ocean" remark in high school can be better appreciated, and any alarming faux pas— such as the groom's father's ringing declaration that "I'm sure we'll all grow to love Susan"—are more easily glossed over.)

Nor is giving a toast at the reception the time for a maudlin display of emotion.

Or the time to go into a long—actually, *awfully* long—reminiscence about something that happened to the bride when she was just a little thing.

Or the time inappropriately to upstage the person who's just made an inappropriately weepy tribute.

Instead, please observe the following:

WHEN IT'S OKAY TO HAVE THE TOASTS: **As soon as** (but not before) the receiving line is over and everyone has a glass to raise. Also, right before the meal, between courses, after the meal—in short, all throughout the reception.

WHO GIVES THE FIRST TOAST: **The best man.** This is one of his chief duties and why he has that strained, nervous look —even if he's in the business and recently tried out his standup material at The Comedy Store.

WHO ABSOLUTELY MUST GIVE A TOAST: **The best man and the groom.** In addition, it's pretty common for the bride to say something nice about the groom and her new in-laws, and to thank her parents. After that, any or all of the attendants may put in a few words. Then the rest of the guests.

WHAT TO SAY IN A TOAST: **Tell who you are** vis-à-vis the bride and groom and wish them well in the future. Do it in your own style—maybe you want to repeat something they once told you, or maybe you want to offer a line of poetry, or maybe there's a fond memory you really do need to reveal—but avoid getting carried away.

MEMORABLE TOASTS: **The ones that emphasize the unity** of two individuals, two families, the larger community. The bride's father who welcomes his guests with talk of being enriched (rather than impoverished) by this wedding is notable. Ditto the groom who remarks on how full his life has become now that he has given it away to another.

WHAT ABOUT THESE TELEGRAMS? **Out-of-town guests** who declined, or got stuck in the snow on the way, or went into labor a week early, often send heartfelt messages to the bride and groom on their special day. (*Note:* If you're a declining out-of-towner, *always do this.*) The best man reads the telegrams after the toasts, either saving them up to do all at once or working them in at various times. If there's a bandleader or DJ, have a chat with him about how to coordinate the stopping and starting.

HOW TO BUY CHAMPAGNE

1 Go to a serious wine merchant, not a grocery store or that place near the beach where you get your kegs.

2 Tell him what your budget is—there are sparkling wines and champagnes for every situation.

3 Order early. If you start far enough in advance, almost any champagne is available to you. Also, you can take advantage of discounts and fluctuating prices. (On the international market, champagne is practically a commodity: prices rise and fall according to demand. For example, the French have been raising their champagne prices to meet the Japanese demand.)

4 Consider having three different wines at the reception, starting with the good stuff for the toasts.

5 When ordering in quantity, comparison shop, negotiate, and ask for a case discount (usually about 10 percent).

6 Figure approximately a half bottle per guest.

7 But remember: not only is the worst thing that can happen to a wedding an after-party catastrophe, but also in almost all states the host can be fined and/or arrested for allowing guests to drive while intoxicated.

8 Make arrangements, if possible, to return unopened, unchilled wine bought in bulk. If not for cash, then for credit.

9 Reflect upon Oscar Wilde, who said: "If I had my life to live again the only thing I would do different is drink more champagne."

BEST FROM THE WEST

An insider's tip *(from Deborah O'Flynn, co-owner of the California Wine Merchants Store, in San Francisco, following her own wedding):* The Iron Horse Wedding Cuvée is a superb champagne. Developed at the Iron Horse Vineyards in California by owners Audrey and Barry Sterling to celebrate their daughter's wedding, it's salmon-colored, affordable, and among the very best of the California sparklers. It has been on the market since only 1985, but is available nationwide. Grab it.

The Best Champagne

TOP FOUR CHAMPAGNES IN THE WORLD

1 Salon
2 Krug
3 Bollinger R.T.
4 Taittinger

TOP CHAMPAGNE FROM CALIFORNIA

Schramsberg

TWO CHAMPAGNES WITH GREAT CALL

Cristal
Dom Pérignon

TWO COMPLETELY DEPENDABLE CHAMPAGNES

Perrier-Jouët
Mumm

AFFORDABLE CHAMPAGNES THAT ARE GETTING BETTER AND BETTER

All the ones from Spain

THEY USED TO BREAK THE CAKE OVER YOUR HEAD

History Marches On, Sort Of

 erhaps you are convinced you know a good wedding cake when you see it (as you will be doing for years to come, in the photos). But do you know why it looks as it does, and in fact what it is—the edible evolutionary replacement for a primary fertility object? Some history:

The early Romans prepared a loaf of barley bread. The groom ate some and then broke the rest over the bride's head to signify the breaking of her hymen and also his dominance over her. Then the guests scrambled for the leftover crumbs to take home as stimuli for their own fertility. The couple was not considered married until they had eaten together, a belief that may linger today, considering that at most weddings the bride and groom feed each other in what would otherwise be a pretty silly display.

At Anglo-Saxon weddings, the bread was replaced by small, hard biscuits.

In medieval times, the biscuits were replaced with small, sweet buns, which were brought by the guests and stacked in a high mass in front of the newlyweds. The couple tried to kiss over the mound and, if they were successful, assumed they would have lots of children.

But the really big moment in cake history came during the Restoration, in the seventeenth century, when Charles II, returning to England from exile in France, brought some French chefs with him. These pastry wizards started icing the solid squares of the bun cake together with a crust of hardened sugar, and after that it seemed nothing to top the whole affair with toys and figures (which once again put everyone in mind of the couple's future children). Eventually, for a grand feast, there were three or more tiers. *Voilà!* (as the French pastry chefs must all have said): the wedding cake that today's brides recognize as theirs had been created.

The Seven Most Desirable Qualities in a Wedding Cake

 ike the gown, the cake is an item the bride may have pictured in her mind for years; now, it is time to move from conception to confection. The price range on cakes is wide: expect to pay anywhere from just under $500 to just over $1,500 for three tiers for 150 guests. The current trend is away from those little Governor Thomas E. Dewey-and-his-bride figures on top. They have been replaced by Superman and Wonder Woman, or by flowers—sugar or candied. If you can't afford an artist working in the mixed media of batter and spun sugar, look for a quality baker who separates his eggs, doesn't use a mix, and will try to express your deepest wishes. And don't use fresh flowers as decorations—they're sprayed with insecticides.

According to leading bakers around the country, the perfect cake has almost the same qualities as the perfect bride:

1 DELICIOUSNESS. Conventional wisdom says this is not as important as the outward beauty of the cake, but the new wisdom says oh yes it is. If it's not delectable it won't seem special to you or, by implication, to anyone else. Think of your wedding cake as a metaphor for your marriage, or the self, and get it right through and through.

2 LIKABILITY. On the other hand, curb the impulse to serve a zucchini creation even if you love it—it's going to be too weird for the out-of-town guests. Remember: the goal is to have most people so thrilled about your cake that they actually eat it. Flavors most people adore include lemon, apricot, chocolate hazelnut, butter rum, almond, orange, chocolate spice, Grand Marnier, mocha rum, pralinée, and many more. Especially beloved in the South is a really good fruitcake laced with brandy, candied fruit, and rich nuts. Carrot, which enjoyed a heyday in the eighties, is still in vogue, although possibly on the way out.

3 YOUTH. If the cake was made ten days in advance of the wedding so the baker could get a jump on decorating it, it's just not fresh. It's old. And dry. And gross.

4 BEAUTY. Mostly, the cake should look as though it belongs at your wedding—and then it will definitely belong in your pictures. To make your work of art site-specific, take a snapshot of the reception area to the baker, and proceed from there. The cake should set off your surroundings, and the snapshot will give you talking points: the color of the oriental rug at the hall, the Art Deco design of the hotel, the fall foliage at the farm. An all-white cake can be dramatic against a colorful background; a cake iced in pastels and adorned with flowers (use silk or bisque if you can't manage spun sugar or candied) can bring wonder to a plain room. And has everyone seen the incredible edible gold leaf that's now available?

5 BALANCE. Are you serving other chocolate desserts? Then don't have a chocolate wedding cake. Is your reception to be in an outdoor garden? Then don't have a lavish construction that would be better in the Pierre Hotel ballroom.

6 ORIGINALITY. Start from scratch. Most bakers will show you slides or photos of their previous creations, which may indeed give you ideas, but putting your own personal stamp on this thing is part of the divine right of brides. Talk about what you want and then let the baker do his stuff. You don't have to go

as far as the woman who was marrying an art professor and insisted her cake resemble the still life in a Flemish painting—but why not?

7 PRESENCE. The finished extravaganza should be no less than the centerpiece of the reception—a contrivance to marvel over. Maybe it's covered in sweeps of flowers; maybe it's topped with whimsically designed bowknots or butterflies or fruit; maybe it's adorned with scrolls and dots and other fancywork; maybe it is not just architecturally significant but also constructed from sheet cakes to keep the cost down; maybe, shockingly, it's chocolate inside and out. Whatever the case, the cake is definitely spectacular. Display it all during the reception, so people can walk around it and look at it and talk about it and just generally feel happy about it. The trend is away from bringing it in near the end of the reception, even with a trumpet fanfare. For one thing, that practice is not historically correct. For another—well, who can wait?

THE GROOM'S CAKE

In the United States, the custom of baking a second, smaller but tastier, wedding cake has mostly faded away; still, it was popular in the United States well into the twentieth century, and even today many southern brides continue such variations on the tradition as reserving a rich chocolate cake to share with their first guests when they return from their honeymoon. Unlike the decorative "bride's" cake, which was to be consumed at the reception, the dense and rich *groom's cake* was torn into pieces to be saved: the morsels were passed through the bride's wedding ring for luck and fertility, and then wrapped in festooned boxes for the departing guests to take home and slip

THE TOP TIER

Among the most inventive artisans in the country, these women custom-make the cakes to die for. Or marry for.

DALLAS/FORT WORTH

Becky Sikes, Ida Mae's Cakes, Box 365, Jacksboro, TX 76056 (817) 567-3439

NEW YORK

Sylvia Weinstock, Sylvia Weinstock Cakes, 273 Church Street, New York, NY 10013 (212) 925-6698

under their pillows. Some believed that the female guest slumbering above her complimentary wedding cake might dream of her own future husband.

KISS THE KIWI GOODBYE

Opting for a Buffet

aced with hundreds of people who expect a wedding meal, it is not imperative to serve a lavish sit-down feast; the buffet is the coming thing. The American palate has become increasingly sophisticated in recent years, however, so make what you do serve dazzling. Skip the caviar and the Dungeness crab legs; forget the giant ravioli and the baby vegetables; omit the black truffle sauce—but be sure the food remains an exciting combination of flavors. Four unpretentious but inspiring buffet menus, gathered from various regions of the country:

From Elizabeth Weddings, Sylvania, Ohio
LAKESIDE BUFFET FOR A MORNING WEDDING

First course	Variety of juices
	Bacon, ham, and vegetable quiches
	Fruits and cheeses
	Home-baked breads, croissants, muffins
Second course	Honey-baked ham
	Potato salad
	Vegetable pasta salad
	Crudités
Dessert	Wedding cake: a homemade cherry cake with very thin buttercream frosting
	Coffee/tea
Champagne	

From Tie-the-Knot Weddings, Palo Alto, California

ENGLISH GARDEN WEDDING BUFFET

First course	Boneless breast of chicken with an herb-cheese filling
	English tea sandwiches
	Salmon mousse
	Pepper tarts
Second course	Crab salad on endive leaves
	Frittata
	Smoked salmon torta
	Cream puffs with curried chicken filling
	Victorian bread basket of cream scones, lemon hearts, and madeleines, served with apricot butter
Dessert	Wedding cake
	Strawberries
	Coffee
Wines	Gloria Ferrer sparkling wine; Edna Valley Chardonnay, Duckhorn Sauvignon Blanc, Pine Ridge Chenin Blanc, Geyersville Red Ridge Zinfandel

From Designer Weddings, Dedham, Massachusetts

NEW ENGLAND CLAMBAKE BUFFET FOR A WEDDING AT THE BEACH

First course	Raw bar
Second course	Steamed clams
	Boiled lobsters with melted butter
	Roasted corn on the cob
	Fresh breads
Dessert	Wedding cake
	Watermelon
Wine	White zinfandel

From the Party Palace, Chattanooga, Tennessee

First course   Cream puffs with warm chicken filling
                  Crudités with spinach dip

Dessert   Bride's cake: yellow pound cake with Bavarian cream filling, iced with rich buttercream
                  Groom's cake: devil's food cake with red raspberry filling and an icing of European chocolate, topped by a gold box filled with fresh grapes and strawberries
                  Hand-painted mints
                  Fresh fruit

Natural fruit punch

203

From food writer and cookbook author Barbara Kafka

MIAMI RESTAURANT WEDDING BUFFET AT HOME

                  Yuca croquettes (from Yuca, a Cuban restaurant)
                  Passion fruit stuffed with crab and shrimp (from Chef Allen's)
                  Tiny quail quarters in a tangerine marinade (from Mark's Place)
                  Green plantain "flowers" with quick-seared tuna (from Chef Allen's)

Dessert   Wedding cake
                  Tropical fruit brochettes
                  Coffee

MYSTERIES OF THE CATERED WEDDING AT HOME REVEALED!

Actress Jane in the Garage with a Crate of Glasses Tells All

Jane Harnick

ane Harnick is a New York–based actress who, when she's not working in television or on the stage, is a waitress for a caterer with clients in New Jersey and the Hamptons. The caterer does a lot of weddings. So does Jane—during the summer of 1990 she routinely worked as many as three a week, moving from one backyard tent in the Tristate Area to another. She says the waiters and waitresses gliding so silently around your wedding are:

• Not actually invisible
• *All* actors
• Usually in love with one another, and have a really good time

together in the car, van, or bus coming out
• Never quite accustomed to changing into their tuxedoes and signature burgundy bow ties in your basement or hilariously incommodious maid's room
• Using the Port-O-Sans instead of the bathroom, by order of your mother
• Getting only about a ten-minute break, well into the reception when things have calmed down, when they sit in the garage, usually on a crate of glasses, eating the leftover food
• Making a very nice living doing this work

Jane says the guests are:
• Starved. The line at the buffet table is a mile long; all anyone wants to do at the beginning of a reception is eat
• Rude, but not as obnoxious or gross as they might be in a restaurant

She says the mother-of-the-bride often appears:
• Bossy—for example, she wants every course presented to the bride and groom before anyone else is served, and it's *really important*
• Clinically insane
• Drunk

She says the most popular buffet includes:
• Avocado vinaigrette
• Assorted pastas
• Chilled salmon with cucumber and dill sauce
• Fillet of beef
• Roasted eggplant, peppers, and onions
• Tons of bread

Jane's favorite moments and memories:
• The time the sun went down on the barn theme wedding, which was actually being held in a barn, and everyone started to freeze to death. The guests, who were intoxicated by then, didn't care so much, but the waiters and waitresses, who are fired on the spot if they take so much as a sip of alcohol on the job, did. So they put on sweatshirts under their tuxedoes—probably the guests never even noticed—and were the hulk waiters.
• The Hawaiian theme wedding when they wore Hawaiian shirts instead of their tuxedoes (which they're sick of anyway).
• The waitress and waiter who were so in love they got married.

A TRIP TO
TONY 'N' TINA'S WEDDING

Tony 'n' Tina's Wedding is the long-running Off-Broadway show that asks the audience to be guests at a typical Italian wedding. It's different every time it's performed because it's so interactive. The show will run in New York, Atlantic City, and elsewhere throughout 1992. A friend writes:

I saw Tony and Tina get married in a church in Greenwich Village in New York. It was Tuesday night, after work. It appeared that several people had come straight from the office because many of the women being led down the aisle, by ushers dressed in tuxedoes and two-tone ruffled shirts, wore suits and sneakers and carried attaché cases.

Robert Cea and Kelly Cinnante, stars of the New York production

The best man has sunglasses, chewing gum, an earring; he just keeps acting really loose. There's a tiny Sicilian grandmother, too, dressed all in black. And a trampy girlfriend for the widowed father of the groom. And Michael, who comes in late—apparently from rehab. The bridesmaids wear red—and chew more gum. One bridesmaid is fat, one is a flirt; and one is pregnant. A sister of the bride is a nun, so she leads everyone in singing. The priest delivers a sermon called "You Are the Church" and assures the couple that love endures even through bad times, which he then proceeds to promise them. The best man plays the guitar and sings "The Wedding Song." The best is the videographer. He's everywhere: backing down the aisle, backing up the aisle, backing into thin air. During the vows he shouts from the nave, "Tony, can you speak up? I'm not getting any audio."

PHOTO BY CAROL ROSEGG COURTESY OF TONY 'N' TINA'S WEDDING AND DAVID ROTHENBERG ASSOCIATES

After the ceremony, we walked through the streets to the reception. It was above a restaurant, in a space just like a catering hall. I was seated at a table of strangers; quickly, we established that we all knew the same G.O. at Club Med, even though some of us had met him at Turquoise and some at Huatulco. A lot of things happen during the reception (dancing, fighting, drinking, and comedy stylings come to mind), but largely you have to deal with your table. In my case, that turned out to be fun because some of them had already been to this wedding (if you take my meaning) and were experts at what was going to happen next. Myself, I don't want to give away the plot, but keep your eye on Dad's girlfriend.

If you find tackiness funny, or if you love it when guys call you "babe" and "gorgeous," this evening has not just Tony's and Tina's names, but yours, all over it. The truth is anyone can have fun at this wedding. You can go by yourself or with your friend(s), or with a date, or in a group, or with your spouse (it's a great anniversary present). I saw old people, middle-aged people, young people. I didn't see any children—which I didn't realize until after I was home, wondering how long it would take for the champagne and baked ziti to wear off.

Speaking of which, you may wonder where Tony and Tina went to recover. Answer: to the Poconos and the heart-shaped bathtubs —or so we were told. By the time the lights went out on the reception, the couple was gone. In ways, that was a shock. They'd had such a memorable wedding, you could almost picture it going on forever. Or the next night. In fact, I could see their wedding lasting for years, a sort of turn-of-the-century *Fantasticks*. For more information about *Tony 'n' Tina's Wedding*, write: David Rothenberg Associates, 1501 Broadway, New York, NY 10036.

Shrink Think 4

What's your best friend going through now that you're married? You couldn't really talk at the wedding. Now is a good time, though, for psychotherapist Karen Faircloth to set down her ideas. And you thought dealing with your family's ego was tricky!

Dear Therapist Karen:

At the rehearsal dinner the night before my wedding, my best friend managed to reveal, strictly in confidence, a piece of gossip that still has me reeling. I was even thinking about it during the ceremony! Part of me is annoyed she sprung such a juicy tidbit so close to the most important day of my life; another part of me is annoyed she waited that long. My husband says forget it, and forget her. What do you say?

A Friend Forever

Dear Friend Forever:

The nice thing about best friends, as you indicate by your signature, is that they do go on forever, and the friendship itself can take many forms (maybe we're talking about marriage too). I say give your thinking some time. What's your hurry to make a decision about your friend? You seem thoughtful: mull this over. (By the way, maybe your husband said what he said because he's already sick of hearing you talk about this. Do you need to practice some containment and private processing? Just a thought.)

Until later,
Karen

WHAT'S THE DAMAGE?

Value endures, but in a roller-coaster economy, prices change. Compare what you are paying by guessing which actual documented costs below were the going prices in 1991. Answers at the bottom.

1 At New York's Bachrach studio, a photographer will spend five hours at your wedding and produce a leather-bound album with forty 8″ x 10″ prints, plus one parent album and one 8″ x 10″ enlargement for ——.
   (a) $500   (b) $850   (c) $1,425

2 Dav El Livery has offices all over the country. In Boston, a three-hour package includes pickup at the bride's home, the trip to the ceremony site, the trip to the reception site. In 1991, to hire a stretch Lincoln limousine with oriental carpeting, moon roof, dry bar, a TV set and VCR cost ——plus gratuity.
   (a) $300   (b) $150   (c) $500

3 The ballroom of the Ritz-Carlton Hotel in Boston is often transformed into a wedding bower by Cambridge's Dutch Flower Garden. The balcony is greened. Trees are brought in. Flowering plants are set about. And on the tables? Centerpieces of peonies and tulips that, depending on lavishness and time of year, can range anywhere from ——to ——apiece.
   (a) $15 to $40   (b) $50 to $150   (c) $200 to $250

4 Once a year, Creative Cakes, in Washington, D.C., bakes the President's birthday cake, but the rest of the time it specializes in wedding cakes. The cost of the cake is figured according to the number of servings. Each serving slice is one inch wide, two inches deep, and three and a half inches high. Slice price? It starts at ——.
   (a) 75 cents   (b) $10.00   (c) $2.50

5 A case of Michel Tribaut Brut champagne at San Francisco's California Wine Merchants is ——figuring the case discount but not the tax.
   (a) $57.98   (b) $129.60   (c) $400.00

6 If you feel you have been taken to the cleaners, imagine what your wedding dress is going through! The cost of drycleaning a gown for storage runs anywhere from $10 to $15 at Bob White Cleaners in Bloomfield Hills, Michigan. They will hang the dress in a special bag that is sealed at the top and bottom and smells of cedar. Or, for only ——, they will sell you a storage box they believe is far superior.

(a) $15   (b) $5   (c) $25

Answers: 1.c; 2.b; 3.b; 4.c; 5.b; 6.a

Putting It All in Perspective 4

• A Viking wedding feast generally lasted about a month.

• Terrace on the Park, a catering establishment in Queens, New York, holds 1,500 cars in its parking lot.

• Princess (now Queen) Elizabeth's wedding cake was nine feet high and weighed five hundred pounds.

• Jewish tradition specifies a short retreat for the just-married couple before taking on the rigors of the feast.

• In Bermuda, the bride and groom have separate wedding cakes. The bride's has a tiny cedar tree which is transplanted after the wedding to symbolize the growth of the couple's love. The groom's cake has a gold leaf, for prosperity.

• At a western-style wedding, the best man is apt to pass around his boot, to collect money for the newlyweds; at some ethnic weddings, the "money dance" is performed—paper money is pinned to the bride and groom by the wedding guests.

• Weddings in the United States make for an annual $30 billion industry, according to estimates. That's *billion*.

• For Grover Cleveland's White House wedding to Frances Folsom (see American History, page 30), the East Room was decorated with bowls of flowers bearing little flags with such mottoes as "God Bless the Supreme Court." There was also a floral creation in the shape of a three-masted schooner labeled the *Hymen* (for the god of love).

• Two touching examples (guaranteed actually to have occurred) of crass paternal excess at a wedding reception: (1) Father engaged chefs from leading restaurants in three cities to prepare three courses of the feast; (2) Father bought out remaining world supply of a wine bottled in 1845 and served all of it to the guests.

Chapter Seven

THE
GETAWAY

BEING

AND

BECOMING

CROSSING THE THRESHOLD INTO THE UNKNOWN

ll through your engagement and wedding, you were encouraged to reinterpret the symbolism of the ages to suit your own needs and style. It has been suggested that marriage too is change incarnate—that as a spouse you move from one existence to another.

Back in the time of marriage by capture, they acted it out: the groom carried the bride away and hid her for thirty days, while the moon went through all its phases and they drank a potion made of honey (thus, the "honeymoon"). And for centuries, wedding guests have demanded proof that the bride and groom were now different: they were apt to follow the bridal couple right into the wedding chamber and scuffle for the bride's loosened clothing, or wait beneath the window until a bloodied sheet was displayed.

Today, there are still some places, including parts of the South in our own country, where the newlyweds are chased by members of the wedding who bang pots and sing and carry on all through the wedding night. For most contemporary brides and grooms, however, the pageant ends on a more tasteful note: they simply appear before the throng in their going-away clothes, pass through a storm of rice, and speed off.

Newlyweds love to honeymoon in Hawaii, Barbados, the Poconos, Niagara Falls, but anywhere they can be alone (it really is better to leave the kids at home) is fine. While you are gone, work together on the age-old question of whether your wedding was the end of childhood or the beginning of adulthood.

However you choose to move from your former self to your new self is up to you and you alone. But do remember this, at this most thrilling and challenging moment of transition: just as weddings forever change but somehow stay the same, so can you.

f every ending is a beginning, it stands to reason that the air around a bride departing her wedding is charged. Also filled with things she is leaving behind and/or escaping forever.

THE BOUQUET. A just-married woman tosses her bouquet with all the determination of someone passing her torch to a new bride—and in fact in pagan times the bouquet *was* a torch. Composed of herbs and garlic to frighten away the evil spirits lingering at the threshold of the bridal couple's new home, it was used to light the first fire therein —after which it was thrown out the door. That a member of the wedding party took to fielding it gave rise to a law of probability that has only gathered force as the centuries have passed: the wedding guest who catches the bouquet will become the next to marry. Some brides make sure their divorced mothers catch their flowers; others bullet the bouquet in the direction of a sister, best friend, or boss. The fix is definitely in, and yet basketball moves in silly dresses is such a fun sport, everyone plays.

THE GARTER. Maybe, in an updating of tradition, the garter at your wedding has already passed to a new groom: either he practically undressed you in front of everybody during the reception to get it, or you demurely surrendered it to him before tossing your bouquet. Or you don't like this custom and refuse to observe it. Whatever the case, the male guest who catches the garter is believed to have won a real prize, and may be the next to marry. The garter-toss dates back to fourteenth-century France. Then, it was the bride herself who did the throwing, and what she threw wasn't her garter but her stocking. Unfortunately, the men all mauled her when she took it off, which is why this act has been refined to the degree it has.

THE RICE. As the bride and groom wave goodbye, their guests respond not only by cheering and making noise (probably to scare away the evil spirits that are lurking about even now), but also by throwing seed-bearing plants. The ritual scattering of rice, nuts, flower petals, and/or fruit has been customary since the earliest times. Some experts believe the practice is merely another effort to secure the bride's fecundity. Others think its origins have to do with the idea that bribing the hovering evil spirits with food may be all that's needed to drive them away. And still others say it's an inducement to the soul to stay (in parts of Indonesia it's believed the bridegroom's soul flies away at the time of marriage). While the professors argue, one thing is certain, though: the bride flees—through hurled rice in the United States, hurled wheat in France, hurled nuts and dates in Greece.

THE SHOES. Maybe they aren't thrown anymore, but men's shoes or boots (or substitute tin cans) are often tied to the back of the getaway car. Why? Because back during marriage by capture, the bride's father became so enraged he ran after the retreating marauders, not only grabbing stones to fling at them, but also snatching off his footwear to throw at their vanishing backs.

"Kay must throw her bouquet!" shrieked Libby MacAusland, stretching on her long legs, like a basketball center, as a crowd of people massed to watch them. "My girl's from Vassar; none can surpass 'er," the radio man struck up. Harald produced two nickels and the newlyweds passed through the turnstile; Kay, who, all agreed, had never looked prettier, turned and threw her bouquet, high in the air, back over the turnstiles to the waiting girls. Libby jumped and caught it, though it had really been aimed at Priss just behind her. And at that moment Lakey gave them all a surprise; the brown-paper parcels she had checked in the hotel proved to contain rice. "That was what you stopped for!" exclaimed Dottie, full of wonder, as the wedding party seized handfuls and pelted them after the bride and the groom; the platform was showered with white grains when the local train finally came in. "That's banal! That's not like you, Eastlake!" Kay turned and shouted as the train doors were closing, and everyone, dispersing, agreed that it was not like Lakey at all, but that, banal or not, it was just the little touch that had been needed to round off an unforgettable occasion.

—*Mary McCarthy,* The Group

DECORATING THE CAR

USE:
- Signs
- Photos
- Flowers
- Crepe-paper streamers
- Tin cans
- Shoes
- Your imagination
- White shoe polish
- Heavy-duty tape

and/or twine (so attachments don't fly around, blocking the driver's vision)
- Soap
- Shaving cream

DO NOT USE:
- Paint
- Balloons (when they pop, they sound like gunshots, which can scare the driver and cause an accident)

DEPARTURE CONVEYANCES THAT ARE
DEPARTURES FROM THE NORM,
BUT POPULAR

1 Team of horses
2 Hot-air balloon
3 Helicopter

4 Vintage fire engine
5 Motorcycle

GRATUITOUS INFORMATION

DID YOU TIP THESE PEOPLE?
Usually included in the fee—if it's not, add 15–20 percent to the bill:
- Caterer or banquet manager
- Bridal consultant

Usually included in the fee—if it's not, distribute gratuity right

after reception:
- Waiters and waitresses
- Bartenders
- Powder room and coat room attendants

Usually 15–20 percent, paid with fee at bride's home just before the trip starts—cash or credit card:
- Limousine driver

TRIED AND TROUSSEAU

 ver since the old days of dowry practices, brides have continued to collect bed and bath accessories, table and kitchen linens, and various garments believed essential to married life. They take these brand-new items with them into marriage—a head start on the fresh start. As late as 1937 in our country, a hope chest might be stocked according to Emily Post's dicta: five sheets for each bed; four pillowcases for each pillow; twelve face towels, three bath towels, four washcloths, and two bath mats per person. The contemporary bride who has not passed her childhood saving washcloths should not despair. Such largess is no longer necessary, and the towels would probably be ruined by the machines in the laundry room anyway.

Similarly, the basic rule for the wardrobe portion of the trousseau (derives from the French *la trousse*, for "little bundle") used to be one dozen of everything; brides might gather together twelve sets of lingerie, twelve tea gowns, twelve smart dresses, twelve pairs of shoes, twelve pairs of gloves. But in a great big Spandex and delicate-cycle world, things are different. All you need to pack:

- a new cross-training outfit
- some really nice lacy underthings
- maybe your bustier
- a power outfit you can wear on job interviews if you're out of work (or looking)

STAY THE SUITE THAT YOU ARE

Arthur Frommer Rates the Honeymoon Destinations

 rthur Frommer has been seeking out value in travel ever since his seminal *Europe on $5 a Day* appeared in the fifties. Today, his book *New World of Travel*, his television program on the Travel Channel, and the proliferation of travel guides bearing his name assure travelers that where there is a will there is a way. Arthur on honeymoons:

"It's important to get away. Don't skip it, and don't stay too close to home, either. Anyone who has just been through the emotions and strain of a wedding needs time to rest and relax— and people beginning a life together need to focus on each other without the usual distractions."

Arthur dismisses certain favored hot spots, to embrace only those places you really want to be. For best deals he advises: plan ahead; shop around; go in the off-season if you can; consult the annual honeymoon guide in the February/March issue of *Bride's*; consider one of the numerous domestic hotel packages; use a travel agent. Taking into consideration a range of budgets, Arthur's own picks and pans:

Six Picks

1 **ROCKRESORTS**. *Caneel Bay, St. John, U.S. Virgin Islands; Rockresorts, Little Dix Bay, Virgin Gorda, British Virgin Islands.* At Caneel, the resort is a peninsula with a necklace of seven beaches. One can be yours alone, and it's landscaped in such a way that you neither see other people nor are seen by them.

PHOTO COURTESY PRENTICE HALL PRESS

Little Dix is on a half-mile crescent of reef-sheltered golden beach; from your terrace, you can watch the pelicans diving. Both Caneel and Little Dix are truly romantic spots, where the day, the night, the future are yours. (*Note:* It is the Rockefeller family who owns these best but not cheap places for a honeymoon.) Little Dix is $4,340 per couple for seven nights from January 1 to March 31; Caneel and other times of year are less costly; three-night packages are available. *For further information and reservations, consult your travel agent or phone Rockresorts at (800) 223-7637.*

A more affordable alternative:

2 MAHO BAY CAMPS. *St. John, U.S. Virgin Islands.* For a fraction of normal hotel costs, you stay in a canvas-sided tent-cottage set on a wooden platform and cantilevered out from the side of a hill lush with foliage; below is a pristine beach. Environmentalist Stanley Selengut designed this setting, and it's definitely back-to-Paradise in character. Says Arthur, you live in a bathing suit at Maho Bay, cook your own meals (although you can eat with others if you prefer), and generally shun the plastic civilization. For activity, you explore underwater life along teeming coral reefs, hike to ruins of eighteenth-century sugar mills, meditate on nature. Off-season May 1–December 14 the rates are as low as $50 per night per couple. *For information, write or phone Maho Bay Camps, 17A East 73rd Street, New York, NY 10021 (212) 472-9453.*

3 SANDALS RESORTS OF JAMAICA. They're in Ocho Rios, Montego Bay, Negril (a new one is opening in Dunn's River, too), and they offer extremely affordable all-inclusive packages—there are even cigarettes on the tables, and you never pay for drinks. White sand beaches, strolling peacocks, the azure Ca-

ribbean, emerald-green mountains, secluded hammocks, coconut palm trees—they're all there to help you rediscover each other. What's more, if you stay at one resort you're allowed to dine, swim, sun at any of the others. (*Note:* These facilities are limited to heterosexual couples—no singles, children, or same-sex couples allowed. It's legal in Jamaica.) *For further information, consult your travel agent or phone (800)-SANDALS.*

4 RENAISSANCE CRUISES. Or almost any cruise line, for that matter. A cruise is a great value these days, largely because there is a glut of cruise ships. As a result, you may be able to pull off a seven-day all-inclusive (even the air fare, from any city in the United States, is thrown in!) package to, say, San Juan, Puerto Rico, at the height of the season for under $1,000 per person; deal with a cruise specialist who can watch for the discounted fares. Arthur singles out the Renaissance line because their ships—to the Far East, the Mediterranean, Europe, Africa, South America, and the Caribbean—are so deluxe, with all-suite accommodations. *For further information, consult your travel agent or phone (800) 525-2450.*

5 BERMUDA. It's usually so expensive it's silly, but if you go between November and March it's affordable. Great tennis, famous golf, and the home of the moped. Putt-putt down country lanes past gardens in bloom all year long. One hundred fifty islands and islets surrounded by pink sand and turquoise water. What could be better? Nothing. *For further information about Bermuda, talk to your travel agent or phone the Bermuda Department of Tourism at (800) 223-6106; from New York (800) 223-6107.*

6 ORLANDO, FLORIDA. If you can observe the dates below and if you avoid the theme parks, you can have a rock-

PHOTO COURTESY MAHO BAY CAMPS

PHOTO COURTESY RENAISSANCE CRUISES

bottom cheap and *fabulous*, time. How? Just use the facilities at any of the almost too-many quality hotels in Orlando—they lower their rates precipitously during those times of year when tourism drops off. Suddenly, it becomes possible to stay in one of the luxury places on International Drive in Disneyland for as little as $30 a night—and to swim, water-ski, play tennis, and dance for free (or very little) right on the premises. As well, zillions of restaurants in the area have low-cost buffets. And the rental car rates are among the lowest in the nation. You are in luck if your wedding coincides with these windows of opportunity: January 6–February 6; May; early June; September after Labor Day–November until Thanksgiving; first three weeks in December. *For further information, contact your travel agent or write the Orlando/Orange County Convention and Visitors Bureau Information Center, Mercado Mediterranean Shopping Village, 8445 International Drive, Orlando FL 32819 (407) 363-5871.*

Seven Pans

1 **THE MEGARESORTS IN HAWAII.** Sometimes called the "wow!" resorts because that's your reaction when you walk into them, these places are built as destinations in themselves. Arthur finds them "cold and forbidding" and says they tend to be patronized by a clientele that appears stunned, even overwhelmed, by such features as motor launches and/or the biggest swimming pool in the state. You won't be comfortable here, he says—but you will be spending a whole lot of money (a three-night honeymoon package may cost $1,200, and the rates are constantly going up). Arthur points to the Westin Kauai at Kauai Lagoons (800-228-3000) as a prime offender.

2 **MEXICO.** The chances are too great that one or both of you will end up with intestinal problems—not nice on a honeymoon.

3 **THE FAR EAST.** Ditto.

4 **EUROPE.** Too expensive. The dollar has dropped so hard it has raised real barriers.

5 **THE POCONOS.** Too demeaning. A bath in a giant glass of champagne?

6 **AUSTRALIA.** Too dull.

7 **SOUTH AMERICA.** Too restive.

Two Otherwise Good Vacations Not Suitable for a Honeymoon

1 SIGHTSEEING. It's too stressful. Unless you've lived together forever and see your honeymoon as just another trip, save it.

2 CLUB MED. There's too much action, and it's too hard to be alone.

THANK YOU A THOUSAND TIMES

---

t may seem like that before you finish. Your mission (whether you choose to accept the gift or return it) is to write a note for every single present you have received—within two weeks if it's before the wedding, and one month if it's after. Good luck!

The wise bride gets in gear as promptly as possible. Such amenities (apologies to Virginia Woolf) as a pen that flows, little charming informals, stamps may tap a rich creative vein. If they don't, too bad—one is meant to keep up with one's thank-you notes no matter what. It's like bill paying: thirty days is okay; sixty days is stretching it; ninety days is old. Real old.

Every writer fears the blank paper, of course, especially when it's crucial to say something nice about wind chimes or a candy dish. To allay anxiety, observe the guidelines (apologies to Strunk and White) below. Ask your husband to help, if you wish—that's very modern. But remember: you're not allowed to type or word-process, no matter how great an author (or secretary) you are. Or he is.

1 Be specific about the gift, especially your impression of what it is. "Thanks for the egg coddlers!" is one of the bravest sentences ever written.

2 Don't use words you would never normally use. (Unless the words are "egg coddlers," of course.)

PHOTO COURTESY CRANE AND CO.

3 Plan what you intend to say before you start writing. A good thank-you note talks about the gift, your gratitude, your spouse, your happiness, and your delight in the gift-giver—all in the space allotted.

4 Try not to load down the note with a lot of adjectives and adverbs—they sound lazy and false, almost as though you were lying.

5 Avoid long, involved sentences. The reader gets into the middle of one of those things and fears he will never get out. You want to thank him? Then do him a favor: be succinct. With a little forethought, a simple statement about a Dutch oven is not that hard to formulate. Really.

6 Skip the clichés. A fresh view on dinner plates marks the wider vision.

7 *Do* tell how you may spend the money received as a gift.

8 *Don't* tell you returned the gift.

9 Tear the note up and start over if it's lifeless or just awful in other ways. After all, the eventual reader stood around the Bloomingdale's gift department trying to get waited on just so she could give you this pasta maker. The least you can do is be articulate.

What's your husband going through as you approach your technical wedding night? Psychotherapist Karen Faircloth knows all about performance anxiety and she's not worried a bit. Maybe that's because she knows your husband isn't either? A recent survey found the thing couples worry about most on their wedding night is lack of finances.

Dear Therapist Karen:
  Is there anything you know that I don't about my husband's mind? Something special I should be alerted to as I set off on my honeymoon, and life, with him?

Just Married

Dear Just Married:
  Studies show that newlyweds are more worried about economic performance than sexual performance. Often, sexual performance has already been established before the wedding ceremony, so concentrate on open communication around decisions that should be bilateral—many of these are economic ones. Right from the beginning, vow to yourself to be open without deviousness, to negotiate with your partner, and to listen to his view without rushing in to "fix" the problem. If you are steady within yourself you never need to be "alerted": you can trust yourself when the situation arises.

Faithfully,
Karen

The honeymoon destination is usually kept a secret until the couple leaves, but now it can be told. Match the famous couple with the sometimes curious, sometimes obvious, sometimes expedient place they went right after their wedding. (*Note:* Islands appear popular.) Answers at the bottom.

The Honeymooners
1 Michael and Kitty Dukakis
2 Prince Charles and Princess Diana
3 Tom Cruise and Nicole Kidman
4 Maury Povich and Connie Chung
5 Caroline Kennedy and Ed Schlossberg
6 Mick Jagger and Jerry Hall
7 Roseanne Barr and Tom Arnold
8 George and Barbara Bush
9 Dan and Marilyn Quayle

The Destinations
(a) Telluride, Colorado
(b) Hawaii
(c) Orange County, Indiana
(d) Isle of Malta
(e) Sea Island, Georgia
(f) Nantucket
(g) Bali
(h) Manhattan

REUTERS/BETTMANN

Answers: 1.f; 2.d; 3.a; 4.h; 5.b; 6.g; 7.b; 8.e; 9.c

PHOTO COURTESY LYDIA MAY STUDIOS, CAMBRIDGE, MASSACHUSETTS

• Once she was over the threshold of her new home, the bride in ancient Greece was presented with a sieve, a coffee roaster, and a pestle as the insignia of her new domestic duties.

• Rather than allowing the wedding celebration to fizzle to a close, some Jewish feasts include *benching*, the chanting of four benedictions at the conclusion of the festivities.

• Ecology-minded brides furnish their guests with birdseed instead of the traditional rice—it's a self-cleaning product that birds can eat.

• On an "Oprah" show devoted to the topic of wedding disasters, the tale was told of the souvenir video that recorded a theft in progress: the gift money meant for the bride and groom was being pilfered by the bride's father.

Chapter Eight

BRIDESPEAK

AFFORDABLE   *adj.* The mid-range; what most people will actually pay. The bridal industry uses this term in reference to many things—gowns and honeymoons, for example—but it doesn't really apply to anything.

BAND   *n.* The people playing the music from *The Big Chill.* (Also: the thing you and your husband are now wearing, for life. Which gives you chills every time you think about it.)

BLIND EMBOSSED   *adj.* An imprinted embellishment, on raised paper, without the addition of color; makes for an unreadable return address on the flap of the invitation envelope. (Also: what you feel like after too much champagne.)

CHILD   *n.* The girl you're leaving behind. (Also: the baby you'll have as a direct or indirect result of this wedding, which is a major point of the whole endeavor. And: the person who should be seated with his parents if he was invited to the wedding on account of being your only nephew and the ring bearer.)

CHINA   *n.* Plates, saucers, bowls, and other dishes for serving food. The good stuff with your pattern should never be confused with the everyday stuff, which may actually be Melmac. (Also: a faraway country not considered by Arthur Frommer to be a suitable honeymoon destination for Americans.)

COAT OF ARMS   *n.* The family crest. Protocol says use it on your invitation only if your father or another male member of your family is issuing the invitation—otherwise, the coat-of-arms police will come get you.

DECKLED   *adj.* With a rough edge. Usually refers more to the paper selected for the invitation than to the best man.

ECRU   *adj.* A color favored by brides for both their invitations and their gowns. Basically, it's off-white or eggshell.

ENSEMBLE   *n.* The wedding invitation and enclosures. (Also: the jazz combo and the bride's going-away outfit.)

FORMAL   *adj.* Describes the wedding with these distinguishing features: invitations are engraved or printed with traditional or personalized wording; at least one hundred guests; bride wears a long gown with a chapel or sweep train; two or six bridesmaids in long or tea-length dresses; groom and his attendants in formal attire (black tie for evening); reception with food and drink. Only slightly more toned down than ultraformal (see below).

GIFT   *n.* Historically, a token of appeasement; currently, an item the bride usually doesn't covet or need. Its sale helps to keep the economy going, though, and presumably someone put some effort into its selection, so think twice about returning it—and whatever you decide, write a thank-you note.

HUNDRED   *n.* The standard unit of measure, as in the number of dollars to leave as a deposit on your dress, the hall, your bouquet, the limo, et cetera. Further: guests come by the hundred; things cost hundreds of times what anyone expected; there are one hundred minor islands (many of them suitable for your honeymoon) in the Hawaiian chain; you may (or may not) have received one hundred proposals—but only one that matters.

I   *pron.* As in you, and the royal we. It's your day.

INFORMAL   *adj.* Describes a wedding held during the day, at any site, including city hall. Handwritten or personal invitations are extended to fewer than fifty guests. The bride wears a suit or cocktail-length dress, and has one honor attendant in a suit or cocktail-length dress. The groom and best man wear business suits. The reception is at home or at a restaurant. (Also: folded, engraved stationery used by some brides for thank-you notes.)

J.J.   James Joyce. Nora Barnacle didn't take on his second initial for her own name until long after he'd said yes I said yes I will Yes.

KEY   *adj., n.* Crucial, as in the selection of your dress, your attendants, the colors of the wedding, the band, the food, your groom, your lawyer. (Also: the thing they give you when you check into your honeymoon hotel that opens the door to your room and a lifetime of happiness.)

LEG-OF-MUTTON   *adj.* Describes a type of sleeve, also known as a gigot, favored by some brides for their wedding gowns. The sleeve is full and loose from the shoulder, nipped in at the wrist. (Also: a difficult-to-eat cut of meat that is probably not the first choice for a wedding feast.)

MAN   *n.* After the wedding, what you have forever.
MONEY   *n.* After the wedding, what you don't have.

NOSEGAY   *n.* A small bouquet carried by the bride. (See also *tussy mussy.*)
NOTARY   *n.* An official with a rubber stamp and a commission that expires sometime. In a few states a notary can marry you—but check that it's legal where you are before you decide to just go to the newsstand for your wedding.

OFFICIANT   *n.* The person who performs the ceremony. Everyone's always embarrassed to ask how much he charges—which varies, but is usually around (natch) one hundred dollars.

PARCHMENT   *n.* Very crisp paper.
PASTILLAGE   *n.* A technique by which a hot sugar compound is pulled out on cold marble, cooled, and formed into decorations. Former White House pastry chef Ann Amernick is famous in Washington, D.C., for making wedding cakes adorned with sweeps of pastillage rose blossoms, in whatever color you'd like.

QUEEN   *n.* The reigning female monarch; the goddess; you. It is impossible to go overboard with this concept.

RICE   *n.* What non-ecology-minded guests throw at the bride and groom as they leave the church. (Also: a type of paper used in wedding ensembles chosen by brides who wish to strike an alternative note and may also have considered printing their invitations on scented or translucent paper or glass.)

SATIN   *n.* A shiny fabric traditionally favored by brides, although at present losing out somewhat to silk. (Also: a shiny paper used for invitations.)
SEMIFORMAL   *adj.* Describes the wedding with the following characteristics: engraved or printed invitations; fewer than a hundred guests; bride wears a floor-length or street-length dress and a headpiece with or without a short veil; one or two bridal attendants in street-length or cocktail-length dresses; groom and

attendants in dark suits and ties; reception with simple refreshments.

SERIF *n.* A type style whose letters have distinctive curls, not the brunette bridesmaid whose last name you never caught. Because serifs are hard to read, *sans serif* styles (without the curls) are often preferred for invitations.

STAKE *n.* A four- to five-foot piece of lumber (don't settle for the inferior twelve to eighteen inches) used to anchor a tent housing 150 people. (Also: the up to $30,000 your father has invested in this shindig.)

SWEETHEART *n.* A scooped neckline resembling the top half of a heart—favored by many brides for their wedding gowns. (Also: of all the pet names your groom has for you, just about the only one he can call you in public.)

THERMOGRAPHY *n.* A printing process less expensive than engraving, with the almost identical effect; involves a resinous powder compound, ink, and heat, and results in raised lettering that is perfectly appropriate for ultraformal and formal wedding invitations.

THRESHOLD *n.* The door jamb your groom carries you over— in part because grooms have done so since Roman times, and in part to symbolize the transition from your old, childish life to your new, highly mature married one. (Also: the level of pain caused by your special white satin shoes that, when you reach it, will allow you to scream in the receiving line.)

TUSSY MUSSY *n.* A small bridal bouquet made from tightly bunched buds and blossoms and resembling a pomander ball; especially popular during Victorian times, which are especially popular now. (Also: the tiffy wiffy you had with the hussy wussy who dated your groom.)

ULTRAFORMAL *adj.* Describes the big blowout, in all its ramifications: the engraved or thermographed invitations in traditional wording; the at least two hundred guests; the bridal gown with cathedral or chapel train; the four to twelve bridesmaids in floor-length dresses; the groom, guests, and ushers in formal attire (which means white tie and tails after 6:00 P.M.); the sit-down meal. Formal (see above) taken a giant step beyond.

VELLUM *n.* An extraordinarily thick paper, preferred for ultraformal and formal invitations.

WONDER *n., v.* An event so unusual as to cause amazement—
e.g., your wedding. (Also: what you do when you reconsider
whether you should make this commitment and, later, when you
marvel that it took you so long. Basically: the activity engaged in
by people who want to know who wrote the book of love.)

XYLOPHONE *n.* A musical instrument struck with small
wooden hammers by a xylophonist, who charges seventy-five dollars an hour and a cartage fee and is cheap at the price.

YEOMAN'S SERVICE *n.* The loyal assistance provided by the
best man and all the other groomsmen who fixed it so you not only
did not miss the plane, but also did not have to have the car
repainted.

ZEUS The supreme deity of the ancient Greeks; identified with
the Roman god Jupiter. Modern brides get married just the way
Greek and Roman goddesses did. It's only fair.

ZIP CODE *n.* A system devised to speed mail deliveries. It
doesn't, but if you want the invitation to arrive at all, either add
the ZIP or hand deliver the thing.

ZURICH A city in Switzerland; pop. 428,000. Great chocolate,
mountains, and cuckoo clocks, but don't go there on your honeymoon, says Arthur; all of Europe is just too expensive these days.

ZYGOTE *n.* The cell formed by the union of male and female
gametes; your firstborn; but that's another story. . . .

BIBLIOGRAPHY AND SOURCES

Chapter One

BOOKS

Briffault, Robert, *Marriage Past and Present* (Boston: Extending Horizons Books, 1956).

Brooke, Christopher, *The Medieval Idea of Marriage* (New York: Oxford University Press, 1989).

Clear, Celia, *Royal Children* (New York: Crown Publishers, 1984).

Fielding, William J., *Strange Customs of Courtship and Marriage* (Garden City, N.Y.: Garden City Books, 1960).

Fox, Robin, *Kinship and Marriage* (London: Penguin Books, 1967).

Hibbert, Christopher (ed.), *Queen Victoria in Her Letters and Journals* (New York: Viking Penguin, 1984).

Howard, George Elliott, Ph.D., *A History of Matrimonial Institutions*, Vol. 1 (Chicago: University of Chicago Press, 1904).

Moore, John C., *Love in 12th Century France* (Philadelphia: University of Pennsylvania Press, 1972).

Mullan, Bob, *The Mating Trade* (London: Routledge and Kegan, 1984).

Murphy, Brian, *The World of Weddings* (London: Paddington Press, 1978).

Urlin, Ethel, *A Short History of Marriage* (Philadelphia: David McKay Co., 1914).

Westermarck, Edward, *A Short History of Marriage* (New York: Humanities Press, 1968).

Wood, Edward J., *The Wedding Day in All Ages and Countries* (New York: Harper and Bros., 1869).

Chapter Two

BOOKS

Joyce, James, *Ulysses* (New York: Random House, 1934).

MAGAZINE AND NEWSPAPER ARTICLES

Glaberson, William, "Love May Not Last, But Litigation Is Forever," *New York Times*, December 9, 1990.

Orth, Maureen, "What's Love Got to Do with It?" *Vanity Fair*, December 1990.

"Slave Wench to Wife: 10,000 Years of the Wedding," *Jewelers' Circular Keystone*, May 1968.

Smolowe, Jill, "What Price Love? Read Carefully," *Time*, October 15, 1990.

Vogel, Carol, "Wedding Bands," *New York Times Magazine*, January 27, 1991.

PAMPHLETS

Levi, Karen, *The Power of Love: Six Centuries of Diamond Betrothal Rings* (London: The Diamond Information Centre, 1988).

Chapter Three

BOOKS

Bride's editors, Bride's *Wedding Planner* (New York: Ballantine Books, 1990).

Emrich, Duncan (ed.), *The Folklore of Weddings and Marriage* (New York: American Heritage Press, 1970).

Garvin, Kristina, *The Message of Marriage* (El Paso, Texas: Weatherford Publications, 1989).

Seligson, Marcia, *The Eternal Bliss Machine—America's Way of Wedding* (New York: William Morrow Co., 1973).

Spence, Annette, *Your Wedding* (New York: Fireside/Simon & Schuster, New York, 1987).

Tasman, Alice, *Wedding Album* (New York: Walker, 1982).

MAGAZINE AND NEWSPAPER ARTICLES

Cook, Anthony, "The $60,000 Wedding," *Money*, May 1990.

Crosby, Connie Crandall, "Collecting Special Memories: The Romance of Hope Chests," *Bridal Guide*, November/December 1990.

Dullea, Georgia, "For the Bachelorette, a Wilder Last Fling," *New York Times*, May 13, 1990.

Gelman, Amy, "Down the Aisle, Surprised," *New York Times*, January 7, 1991.

Gummer, Scott, "Always a Bridesmaid," *Life*, June 1990.

Krauss, David, "Here Comes the Bride," *Modern Bride*, February/March 1991.

Nemy, Enid, "Planning a Wedding, and the Pitfalls of an Invitation List," *New York Times*, July 15, 1990.

"19 Hottest Businesses for 1990," *Entrepreneur*, December 1989.

"Planning Your Guest List," *Bridal Guide*, November/December 1990.

"Weddings of the Rich and Famous," *National Enquirer*, special issue, 1990.

"Your Marriage License," *Modern Bride*, February/March 1991.

Chapter Four

BOOKS

Cunnington, Phillis, and Catherine Lucas, *Costume for Births, Marriages and Death* (London: A. & C. Black, Ltd., 1972).

Monserrat, Ann, *And the Bride Wore . . .* (New York: Dodd, Mead Co., 1973).

MAGAZINE AND NEWSPAPER ARTICLES

Schiro, Anne-Marie, "Fantasy and Taste in a New Bridal Salon," *New York Times*, September 5, 1990.

Vaughen, Michelle, "Wedding Belles," *New York Times Magazine*, January 27, 1991.

Chapter Five

BOOKS

Diamant, Anita, *The New Jewish Wedding* (New York: Summit Books, 1984).

Eklof, Barbara, *With These Words . . . I Thee Wed* (Boston: Bob Adams, Inc., 1989).

Munro, Eleanor, *Wedding Readings* (New York: Viking, 1989).

Nash, Ogden, *Verses from 1929 On* © 1943 by Ogden Nash. First appeared in *Cosmopolitan*. Reprinted by permission of Little, Brown and Co.

New York Public Library, *Desk Reference*, Webster's New World (New York: Simon & Schuster, 1989).

MAGAZINE AND NEWSPAPER ARTICLES

"License to Wed," *Bridal Guide*, November/December 1990.

Chapter Six

BOOKS

Ellfeldt, Lois, *Folk Dance* (Dubuque, Iowa: W. M. C. Brown Co., 1969).

Gilbert, Cecile, *International Folk Dance at a Glance* (second edition) (Edina, Minn.: Burgess Publishing Co., 1974).

Kraus, Richard, *Folk Dancing: A Guide for Schools, Colleges, and Recreation Groups* (New York: The Macmillan Company, 1962).

Loring, John, with Patricia Warner, *The Tiffany Wedding* (New York: Doubleday, 1988).

New York Public Library, *Desk Reference*, Webster's New World (New York: Simon & Schuster, 1989).

Tolle, Leon J., Jr., *Floral Art for Religious Events* (New York: Hearthside Press, Inc., 1969).

MAGAZINE AND NEWSPAPER ARTICLES

Fisher, Lawrence M., "Winery's Answer to Critics: Print Good and Bad Reviews," *New York Times*, January 9, 1991.

Kafka, Barbara, "Wedding Bites," *New York Times Magazine*, January 27, 1991.

Chapter Seven

BOOKS

McCarthy, Mary, *The Group* (New York: Harcourt Brace & World, 1963).

About the Author

Jennifer Rogers is a writer living

in Los Angeles. Her stories and

essays have appeared in

Cosmopolitan, Good Housekeeping,

McCall's, New York,

and *Woman's Day.*